CONDITIONS OF MEANINGFUL LIFE

European and International Perspectives

Edited by

Wolf Bloemers and Jürgen Wolf

BoD - Books on Demand
Norderstedt, Germany

Bibliografische Information der Deutschen Nationalbibliothek:
Die Deutsche Nationalbibliothek verzeichnet diese Publikation
in der Deutschen Nationalbibliografie; detaillierte bibliografische
Daten sind im Internet über dnb.dnb.de abrufbar.

Herstellung und Verlag: BoD – Books on Demand, Norderstedt

ISBN: 978-3-7494-4926-2

Contents

Acknowledgements

Many individuals have contributed to this project of documenting the papers of the international conferences in Ukraine 2018. We acknowledge the support of the colleagues of the hosting universities, in particular Lucy Romanenkova and Svitlana Paschenko. We would like to thank Lea Schubert for her assistance in collecting the papers and making first revisions. Brigitte Raschke assisted us during the production process. We are grateful for her clerical expertise and her deep understanding of the intentions of the authors and the editors.

Preface: The History behind this Book Highlights and Beacons

Wolf Bloemers

This book owes its publication to an almost 20-year-long history of intensive collaboration and partnership between numerous universities in the European Union and several universities in Ukraine. I continue to be the initiator and coordinator of these joint efforts, and working with my Ukrainian as well as other European and global academic partners and friends remains a heartfelt passion and honour for me.

So many highlights need to be emphasised: a continuous exchange of students and professors including studies and practical trainings; the teaching of courses on special and inclusive education, psychoanalytical pedagogy as well as on ethics and social justice; several common research projects with regard to social inclusion, focusing on disabled people and giving them a voice; long-lasting and extensive application-oriented projects including children and their parents, students, social pedagogues, administrators, and professors; the development and implementation of the so far only and unique „outpatient socio-pedagogical and special-pedagogical/therapeutic centre" at a Ukrainian university; the publication of several joint scientific books; the development of the joint European Bachelor's (B.A.) programme „European Inclusion Studies" and ten corresponding bi-lingual resource bank books (together with eight European universities), assessed by the European Union as „Best European Practice" and „Best European Model"; the implementation of the European Master's (M.A.) programme „European Perspectives on Social Inclusion", shared by 14 European universities including a

Ukrainian one (ZNU). Common degree examinations of students, and numerous additional activities such as the international conference „Ageing in Europe", held at ZNTU in 2013, not to forget the uplifting, delightful experiences of cross-border thinking, celebrating and enjoying unforgettable hours, weeks and years together!

The latest beacon within this framework of cross-border cooperation was the international conference „Conditions of Meaningful Life – European/International Perspectives" held in May 2018 at the hosting universities Classic Private University (CPU) in Zaporizhzhya and Taras Shevchenko National University (TSNU) in Kyiv, bringing together academics from the European Union, the USA and Ukraine, in order to share and discuss common humanitarian values against the background of a current „world in turmoil" (Reding) and a „world in shards" (Guterres).

Having been asked by many participants of both conferences to publish our contributions we decided to do so in order to disseminate the ideas and results to a wider audience. This volume includes all presentations given at said international conferences. May it serve as further motivation and encouragement for continued reflections, discussions and research on „Meaningful Life"

Meaningful Life in Times of Worldwide Clashes, Tremors and Uncertainties. An Outline of Analysis and of Giving Directions

Wolf Bloemers

1. Flashlights of Topicality – Meaningful Life? What means meaningful?

These are current, oppressive images of our everyday, diverse reality all over the world: examples of meaningful life? If not – why? If yes – useful for whom? Do you wish for yourself and for your fellow human beings quite different representations of meaning in life, or other options – and if so, which ones? What do you mean by „meaningful life"? Is your life meaningful – or is it meaningless or bereft of content? Is that even an issue for you? What does that actually mean: "meaningful life"? And how do you win this?

I would like to trace these questions by cursorily contrasting the subjectively and exemplarily selected photos with the understanding and the concept of meaning, then sketch their context very summarily with some mosaic stones of a currently "invalidated world order" (Steingart 2016, 10), a "world in turmoil" (Reding 2017, 03.12.2017 by Anne Will), a "world in shards", proclaimed „red alert for 2018" (Guterres 31.12.2017) present some sources of meaning of life from current empirical research results and finally try to derive from it some conditions, offers and signposts for personal giving meaning by means of some thought splinters from psychologists.

The images of unemployment, poverty, starvation, civil war, terrorism, migration, ecological devastation, etc. shown above reveal a part of the unfortunately continously growing present reality of people (individuals and groups) as victims, socially dependents, seekers, as outcasts, as the desperate, as the needy, as fleeing from other people, who are pushed either from war, from brutal annihilators/exterminators (IS) or from the so-called social "circumstances", to which they are helplessly delivered, to the edge of a multi-options society, or who have almost been thrown out of its fragile and changing order.

Although we can not ask those affected if they think their lives are meaningful – and I assume they do not – it is true that body language and ambience are quite clearly reflecting despair, distress, misfortune, fear, which can be reckoned as a sign of unfulfilled basic needs sensu Maslow and therefore have lead to the loss or to the inability to own giving meaning and meaningfulness respectively have caused inner void.

Obviously, in all of these examples, one of the essential prerequisites for an individual search for meaning and meaningfulness is lacking: the free choice of one's own life situation, harmonized with others.

In addition, meaningfulness as a fundamental experience of significance is based on a largely unconscious evaluation of one's life as *coherent* (harmonious and appropriate), as *significant* (effectiveness of one's own actions), as *orientated* (content orientation of one's own life and own decision-making) and as *belonging* (self-perception as an integrated and needed part of a larger whole) (see Schnell 2016, 7 f). Since, in my opinion, none of these four interrelated criteria can be found as central elements of meaningfulness in the images shown above, consciously experienced meaning crises or meaninglessness can be assumed here, since disorientation, emptiness, inactive world reference and lack of beeing needed are obvious.

Even if the perception of purpose in life as meaningful or meaningless is always subjective, dynamic and specific, even if the meaning of a certain person in a particular situation is attributed to a matter, to an action or to an event (Schischkoff 1991) and if meaning of life is considered to be a subjective "multi-dimensional construct" of the individual (Schnell 2009, 2014a, 2016, 6), thus if meaning is the result of a subjective assessment process, then this construction, however, always happens in the context of social relations, since the own life-style of a person as a social being is ever realized in relation to others only.

If we also refer the latter body of knowledge to the pictures presented at the outset, then we can assume for all of them that each can be regarded as a document of non-meaningful life due to the disparity of socially desired/propagated basic values and goals (such as satisfaction, well-being, health, justice, security, work and livelihood, social inclusion) on the one hand side, and on the other hand the optically proven, individual non-realizations.

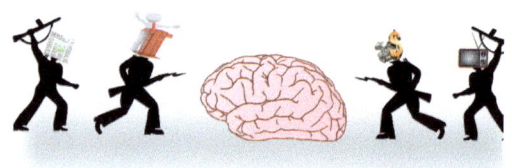

2. Search for Meaning – Frazzling universe, multiple options, research

The question of a sense of life, of a meaningful life, is a teleological one; it is about meaning, purpose, value, benefit, or fulfillment that the individual seeks and attaches to his life in the world and with others. This search is usually carried out in the field of tension between pedagogical, cultural and religious requirements and imprints through education, training and institutions on the one hand, and on the other hand, the demand to lead an autonomous, self-determined life, considered as meaningful in person. Whatever sense of life is followed, wether imposed or chosen or predominantly unreflected, it always updates or loses itself in the current social context, because meaning processes always take place in the confrontation with overarching contexts of the environment, supportively or restrictively acting on the individual.

If this social context experiences cracks, collisions and tremors, a meaningful life lived up to this point is in danger of becoming crisis-shaken or of becoming completely bereft of content and to experiencing a threatening life crisis. In addition to personal crashes, acid life tests, traumas and interrupted continuity of experience such as serious illness, divorce or death of relatives, in addition to exhaustion due to overburdening performance and time pressure, in addition to pathogenic living conditions such as alienation, loneliness or lack of financial resources, it is currently the ongoing European and world-wide gigantic upheavals, collisions, tremors, transformation processes and splits of the social connections, which lead to uncertainties and new questions about a meaningful life in a world that has gotten out of joint.

We are currently experiencing *collisions* by the clashes of democratic ideas with ever-increasing ideas and realities of selfish renationalisation (USA, Hungary, Poland, Russia), right-wing populism, Islamism, economic protectionism and authoritarianism (Putin, Erdogan), as well as the growth of parallel societies. All of this splits previous communities, curtails the individual's autonomy and legal certainty, challenges existing social affiliations and sorts them binarily and sanctioning into allegiances and opponents.

We are currently experiencing a global economic, social and our community resources threatening *tremor* due to globalization, digitization, climate change and extreme weather, economic and financial crisis, a new nuclear crisis (North Korea), super germs, terrorism as a kind of "3rd World War" (Steingart 2016) and through numerous civil wars, by which fields of work, living environments, livelihoods and national social structures are destroyed due to power and greed, recklessness, selfishness and high criminality, so that ideals of open and just societies are becoming questionable and repressed and that mass migration and refugee flows fundamentally shatter and change social and social systems.

We are currently experiencing a surge of *uncertainty* through an incredible, bewildering variety of life concepts, depreciation and change in values, disinhibition and hatred in so-called social media, increased manipulation of opinion and influence through fakes, out-of-control electronic spying (NSA) and increasing cybercrime, through media seduction and advertising in the mass media to ever greater consumption, through a growing income gap between rich and poor and with a rapidly rising proportion of poverty and unemployment: all this seeps or pushes into our life spheres. It alters mutual trust, intensifies self-centeredness, causes orientationlessness and bursts social coherence.

These rapid processes of change and enormous structural changes, which massively influence, restrict or question many previous life-senses, i.e numerous, meaningful lives so far, have been a societal theme for quite some time that is controversially discussed, but whose interpretations are hard-fought in the multi-option society. In this sometimes aloof struggle, the lack of transparency and incomprehension regarding the effectiveness as well as the perceived powerlessness of the citizens not being able to change anything and to be a dead duck for a meaningful life perspective, lead to their growing insecurity, to despair, to cynicism, to loss of their own importance, to acute or chronic inability to live, to indifference, often to the flight into drugs, to depression or even to refuse to live with suicide.

However, this feeling of powerlessness and helplessness, this "specter of uselessness" (Sennett 2007) is confronted in the Western world – characterized by super-diversity and functional differentiation –, by an abundance of competing and complementary concepts and sources of meaning as offers for the creation of meaning. Its reception and practical application however depends on factors such as resources, personality traits, marital status, origin, talent, age, etc., and therefore requires quite different propagation and mediation support. In this way, people can experience very different living conditions and goals as meaningful or meaningless, depending on their own needs and living situation (see Schnell 2016, 31), as e.g. revealed by the recruitment of young people in Europe as IS terrorists who consider their lives here meaningless.

To clarify again: life itself has no intrinsic meaning, meaning is always relative, is variable, never inherent to a situation or an idea per se, but is always subjectively deduced from sources and attributed to its own goal-orientation and its own active actions. So people *attribute* sense to *their lives* by using sources that are meaningful to them, which give orientation and from which they draw meaning.

After philosophers, other scientists and religious representatives have tried for hundreds of years to identify the meaning of life and pretend to its followers and have thereby come to a large number of very different statements and results (McCaffrey 2017), now modern psychology has presented detailed and verifiable results by means of empirical research: there is no universal or unique meaning of life but only the meaning each individual choose to give it.

> WE SHOULD GIVE MEANING TO LIFE,
> NOT WAIT FOR LIFE TO GIVE US MEANING
> Stacy

Broad empirical research in the field of Personality and Differential Psychology regarding meaning and meaning of life has identified 26 sources in 5 major dimensions (Lebe, Schnell & Becker 2007), from which people draw meaning for a meaningful life. These are:

Vertical Self-Transcendence	Horizontal Self-Transcendence	Self-Realization	Order	We and Well-being
Explicit Religiosity (3)	*Social Commitment (6*	Challenge	Tradition	*Community (10)*
Spirituality	*Affinity with nature (8)*	Individualism	Down to Earthness	Fun
	Self-knowledge	Power	Morality	Love
	Health	*Development (5)*	Rationality	Wellness
	Generativity (1)	Performance		*Care (2)*
		Freedom		*Conscious Experience (7)*
		Knowledge		*Harmony (4)*
		Creativity (9)		

(I have marked the strongest predicators for meaningfulness in the table in the ranking 1-10 in italics.)

My own short surveys in 2017 and 2018 in the international circle of friends in Germany, Greece, Spain and Portugal (N = 21) on concepts of meaningful life and sources of meaning yielded the following result: *first and foremost mention was health (11), followed by social engagement/active shaping of one´s own life as well as the life of the community/society (8), social and material security and a satisfying safe job (5), freedom & peace (4), family and home (4), followed by love and harmony (3), then by education, friends and children, being needed (2), and at last by living without fear, partnership, self-realisation, mobility (1).*

3. Finding Meaning - Reflections, Preconditions, Examples, Directions

How do we come to a meaningful life in our world, which threatens to come apart at the seams? What needs to be done, what conditions are required, what content can convey meaning? There are different answers to this from different perspectives, which, however, agree in several aspects. In the following, I have chosen some of them subjectively, which in my opinion can be trend-setting and universal.

In everyday life meaning is usually not an issue and is not questioned, but in stressful phases of life, the question of the meaning of one´s own life probably emerges in thinking of every human being who then critically questions his life-touching, relevant events and the meaningfulness of his own actions, doing by that a kind of self-exploration. For this reason, for Hessel (2011) questions of meaning are also the basis of indignation and engagement, from which conscious *consequences/meaningfulness* can emerge.

Ryff and Singer (1998) reveal that meaningful living is possible by „invested and committed living", that is, devoting oneself to a cause that can give meaning to a life, to oblige oneself to it, and to consistently implement it. This means that this decision must be preceded by a conscious, a reflective act, a mental argument that requires self-initiative. Viktor Frankl, the founder of logotherapy, the 3rd Viennese school of psychotherapy, speaks in this context of a "will to the meaning", which is inherent in each human being due to his spiritual dimension, his inner freedom to vote, and which therefore can be detected. "Those who have a why to live endure almost every how". On the basis of this maxim Frankl explored how meaningfulness is possible even in the face of severe blows of fate and enables people to remain mentally healthy in times of crisis. "A why – that is a life content; and the how – those were the circumstances that made camp life so difficult that it was bearable only in terms of a why "(Frankl 2017).

Further conditions for finding one's own meaning and meaningful life are the already mentioned personal freedom as freedom of dissenters and the freedom for one's own choice and self-determination, the before mentioned 4 indispensable criteria: coherence/significance/orientation/social affiliation; furthermore, the feeling of being needed, of importance, as well as mutual respect, recog-nition and affirmation, because we depend for good or for evil on communication and acknowledgement: "In all walks of life people confirm each other (…) in their human qualities and abilities, and a society can be called human to the extent that its members confirm each other" (Buber 1957, 102).

Possible content fields in which meaningful life can be found are – besides those mentioned above in the research results – the family, the work, the profession and the love; "Meaning receives life only through love: that is, the more we are able to love and to surrender, the more meaningful our lives become (Hesse 2008, 7). Other sources of meaning are religious institutions (fraternities), participation in NGOs and in charitable organizations (eg medecins sans frontières), especially the voluntary, non-financially remunerated work.

It is proved that experiencing strong sense of purpose in life of volunteers is higher than that of people without voluntary work (Hoof & Schnell 2009). In addition, there are many, completely new sources of meaning in response to climate change and depletion of resources, such as engagement and taking part in very progressive activities and new ways of life oriented to the common welfare, such as: *Exchanges, Urban gardening or Food-Coops,* and many more besides.

The more tasks and activities are experienced as significant and meaningful, the greater the likelihood of mental, intellectual, physical health. Several studies at the University of Rochester have shown that meaningfulness correlates positively with subjective quality of life and objective life span (see Hill & Turiano 2014 and Schnell 2016, 114). Antonovsky has already demonstrated in 1979 by salutogenesis research that performance of meaningfulness has motivational health, life and stress-coping skills.

Finally, as a possible guideline for finding meaning, I provide you with 4 maxims that the Canadian clinical psychologist Paul Wong has set out as an extract from his research results on meaningful life:

1. You need to choose a worthy purpose or a significant life goal; 2. You need to have sufficient understanding of who you are, what life demands of you, and how you can play a significant role in life; 3. You and you alone are responsible for deciding what kind of life you want to live, and what constitutes a significant and worthwhile life goal; 4. You will enjoy a deep sense of significance and satisfaction only when you have exercised your responsibility for self-deter-mination and actively pursue a worthy life goal (Wong 1998, 140).

However, it must be pointed out very clearly that it is precisely the needy persons and groups shown in the introductory photos (the suspended, the outcast, the globalization losers, etc.) – as well as people with disabilities – who require special personal, financial and institutional support for the search of a meaningful life in order to socially cushion the depressing consequences of globalization and individualization of lifestyles and to offer them new orientations.

And if you want to have a little more funny and simple guideline, see a humourous maxim in Monty Python's sketch comedy movie 'The Meaning of Life,' (1983): At the end of the film a character played by Michael Palin is handed an envelope containing 'the meaning of life,' which he opens and reads out to the audience: *"Well, it's nothing very special. Uh, try to be nice to people, avoid eating fat, read a good book every now and then, get some walking in, and try to live together in peace and harmony with people of all creeds and nations."*

Closing remarks

If you yourself are still looking for a new or another meaning of your own life, I would like to provide you with two suggestions, I found in Tatjana Schnell (2016) and which I consider to be very creative and helpful:

- Keep a *journal of meaning* for a week, make daily notes of your activities and reflect on meaningful and meaningless activities at the weekend;
- or: Think *of your life as a book*, divide it into chapters, and title them (2016,149).

Let me finish by offering you some selected quotations for your consideration:

- The sole meaning of life is to serve humanity. (Leo Tolstoi)
- In our life there is a single color, as on an artist's palette, which provides the meaning of life and art. It is the color of love. (Marc Chagall)
- Life is without meaning. You bring the meaning to it. (Joseph Campbell)
- The meaning of life differs from man to man, from day to day and from hour to hour. What matters, therefore, is not the meaning of life in general but rather the specific meaning of a person's life at a given moment (Viktor E. Frankl)

(**References** at the end of the German version below)

Sinnvolles Leben in Zeiten weltweiter Konflikte, Erschütterungen und Unsicherheiten
Ein analytischer Aufriss und einige Hinweise

Wolf Bloemers

1. Blitzlichter auf Aktualitäten – Sinnvolles Leben? Was heisst „sinnvoll"?

Dies sind aktuelle, beklemmende Bilder aus unserer alltäglichen, vielfältigen Wirklichkeit in aller Welt: Beispiele für sinnvolles Leben? Wenn nein – warum? Falls ja – sinnvoll für wen? Wünschen Sie für sich und für Ihre Mitmenschen ganz andere Darstellungen von Lebenssinn, bzw. andere Optionen – und wenn ja, welche? Was verstehen Sie unter einem „sinnvollen Leben"? Ist Ihr Leben sinnvoll – oder ist es sinnlos oder sinnentleert? Ist das überhaupt ein Thema für Sie? Was heißt das eigentlich: „sinnvolles Leben"? Und wie gewinnt man dieses?

Diesen Fragen möchte ich ein wenig nachspüren, indem ich im folgenden diese subjektiv und exemplarisch ausgewählten Fotos mit dem Verständnis und dem Konzept von Sinn kursorisch kontrastiere, im Anschluss daran ihren Kontext sehr summarisch mit einigen Mosaiksteinen einer derzeit „ungültig gewordenen Weltordnung" (Steingart 2016,10), einer „Welt in Aufruhr" (Reding 2017, 03.12.2017 bei Anne Will), einer „Welt in Scherben" und in „Alarmstufe rot für 2018" (Guterres 31.12.2017) skizziere, einige vorhandene Quellen und Sinnstifter von Lebenssinn aus aktuellen empirischen Forschungsergebnissen aufzeige und abschließend versuchen will, daraus Bedingungen, Angebote und Wegweiser für persönliche Sinngebungen abzuleiten mittels einiger Gedankensplitter aus den Wissensbeständen der Psychologie.

Die zuvor gezeigten Bilder von Arbeitslosigkeit, Armut, Hunger, Bürgerkrieg, Terrorismus, Migration, Umweltzerstörung etc.

offenbaren ein – leider stetig wachsendes – Teil derzeitiger Realität von Menschen (Individuen und Gruppen) als Opfer, als sozial Abgehängte, als Suchende, als Ausgestoßene, als Verzweifelte, als Notleidende, als vor anderen Menschen Flüchtende, die entweder von Krieg, von brutalen Vernichtern (IS) oder von den sogenannten gesellschaftlichen „Umständen", denen sie hilflos ausgeliefert sind, an den Rand einer Multioptions-Gesellschaft gedrängt, bzw. aus deren fragilen und im Umbruch befindlichen Ordnung fast hinausgeworfen worden sind.

Zwar können wir die Betroffenen nicht befragen, ob sie ihr Leben als sinnvoll bezeichnen – und ich gehe davon aus, dass sie das nicht tun –, doch spiegeln Körpersprache und Ambiente recht eindeutig Verzweiflung, Not, Unglück, Angst und Unfreiheit wider, die als Zeichen unerfüllter Grundbedürfnisse sensu Maslow gelten können und daher mit zum Verlust bzw. zum Unvermögen der Fähigkeit zu eigener Sinnsetzung und Sinnerfüllung führen bzw. Sinnleere bewirkt haben.

In allen Beispielen fehlt es hier offensichtlich zunächst an einer der wesentlichen Voraussetzungen für eine individuelle Sinnfindung und Sinnerfüllung: an der freien Entscheidung zur eigenen, mit anderen abgestimmten Lebenssituation.

Hinzu kommt, dass Sinnerfüllung als grundlegende Erfahrung von Sinnhaftigkeit auf einer weitestgehend unbewussten Bewertung des eigenen Lebens als *kohärent* (stimmig, schlüssig und passend), als *bedeutsam* (Wirksamkeit eigenen Handelns), als *orientiert* (inhaltliche Ausrichtung des eigenen Lebensweges und eigene Entscheidungsfindung) und als *zugehörig* (Selbstwahrnehmung als integrierter und gebraucht werdender Teil eines größeren Ganzen) beruht (vgl. Schnell 2016, 7 f). Da sich meiner Auffassung nach keine dieser vier miteinander zusammenhängenden Kriterien als zentrale Elemente von Sinnerfüllung in den gezeigten Bildern wiederfinden lassen, können hier bewusst erlebte Sinnkrisen bzw. Sinnleere angenommen werden, da Orientierungslosigkeit, Leere, inaktiver Weltbezug und mangelndes Gebrauchtwerden offensichtlich sind.

Auch wenn die Wahrnehmung von Lebenssinn als sinnvoll oder sinnleer stets subjektiv, dynamisch und spezifisch ist, auch wenn Sinn von einer bestimmten Person in einer bestimmten Situation einer Sache, einer Handlung oder einem Ereignis beigelegt wird (Schischkoff 1991) und Lebenssinn damit als ein subjektives „multidimensionales Konstrukt" des Einzelnen anzusehen ist (Schnell 2009, 2014a, 2016, 6), wenn Sinn also das Ergebnis eines subjektiven Bewertungsprozesses darstellt, so steht diese Konstruktion doch stets im sozialen Kontext, da sich die eigene Lebensführung des Menschen als soziales Wesen immer nur in der Beziehung zu anderen realisiert.

Beziehen wir auch letzteren Wissensbestand auf die eingangs gezeigten Bilder, so kann bei allen aufgrund der Disparität von einerseits gesellschaftlich propagierten Grundwerten und Zielen (wie: Zufriedenheit, Wohlbefinden, Gesundheit, Gerechtigkeit, Sicherheit, Arbeit und Auskommen, soziales Eingebundensein) und andererseits den hier optisch belegten, individuellen Nicht-Realisierungen angenommen werden, dass letztere als Dokumente von jeweils nicht-sinnvollem Leben angesehen werden können.

2. Sinnsuche – ausfransendes Universum, mannigfaltige Wahlmöglichkeiten, Forschungen

Die Frage nach einem Lebenssinn, nach einem sinnvollen Leben, ist eine teleologische; es geht dabei um die auf einen Zweck, auf ein Ziel, auf einen Wert, auf einen Nutzen oder eine Erfüllung hin ausgerichtete Bedeutung, die der einzelne Menschen für sein Leben in der Welt und mit anderen sucht und ihr beimisst. Diese Suche erfolgt meist im Spannungsfeld zwischen pädagogischen, kulturellen und religiösen Vorgaben und Prägungen durch Erziehung, Ausbildung und Institutionen einerseits, und andererseits der Forderung, ein autonomes, selbstbestimmtes, selbst als sinnvoll erachtetes Leben zu führen. Welchem Lebenssinn auch immer gefolgt wird, ob aufgezwungen oder gewählt oder sehr häufig auch unreflektiert, er aktualisiert oder verliert sich immer im derzeitigen gesellschaftlichen Kontext, denn Sinnprozesse finden stets in der Auseinandersetzung mit übergreifenden Zusammenhängen der Umwelt statt, die unterstützend oder einschränkend auf das Individuum einwirkt.

Erfährt dieser soziale Kontext Risse, Kollisionen oder Beben, dann steht ein bislang sinnvoll gelebtes Leben in der Gefahr, sinnerschüttert oder durch den Sinnverlust ganz sinnlos zu werden und eine bedrohliche Lebenskrise zu erfahren. Neben persönlichen Brüchen, Lebensprüfungen, Traumen und unterbrochener Erlebenskontinuität wie etwa schwere Krankheit, Scheidung oder Tod von Angehörigen, neben Erschöpfung aufgrund von überforderndem Leistungs- und Zeitdruck, neben krankmachenden Lebensbedingungen wie Entfremdung, Vereinsamung oder mangelnden finanziellen Ressourcen sind es derzeit die aktuellen, europa- und weltweiten gigantischen Umbrüche, Kollisionen, Beben, Transformationsprozesse und Spaltungen der gesellschaftlichen Zusammenhänge, die zu Unsicherheiten und neuen Fragen nach einem sinnvollen Leben in einer aus den Fugen geratenen Welt führen.

Wir erfahren derzeit *Kollisionen* durch das Aufeinanderprallen demokratischer Ideen mit immer stärker werdenden Ideen und Realitäten von egoistischer Renationalisierung (USA, Ungarn, Polen, Russland), von Rechtspopulismus, von Islamismus, von wirtschaftlichem Protektionismus und Autoritarismus (Putin, Erdogan) sowie durch das Anwachsen von Parallelgesellschaften. All dies spaltet bisherige Gemeinschaften, beschneidet dem Individuum seine Autonomie und Rechtssicherheit, stellt bisherige soziale Zugehörigkeiten in Frage und sortiert binär und sanktionierend nach Gefolgschaften und Opponenten.

Wir erfahren derzeit ein weltweites wirtschaftliches, soziales und unsere Gemeinressourcen bedrohendes Beben durch Globalisierung, Digitalisierung, Klimawechsel und Extremwetter, durch Wirtschafts- und Finanzkrise, durch eine neue Atomkrise (Nord Korea), durch Superkeime, durch Terrorismus als eine Art

„3.Weltkrieg" (Steinhart 2016) und durch etliche Bürgerkriege, mit denen Arbeitsfelder, Lebensräume, Existenzen und nationale Sozialgefüge aus Macht- und Geldgier, aus Rücksichtslosigkeit, Selbstsucht und mit hoher Kriminalität zerstört werden, Ideale offener und gerechter Gesellschaften fragwürdig und verdrängt werden und Massen-Migration und Flüchtlingsströme Gesellschafts- und Sozialsysteme von Grund auf erschüttern und verändern.

Wir erfahren derzeit stark anwachsende *Unsicherheiten* durch eine unglaubliche, verwirrende Vielfalt an Lebensentwürfen, durch Werteverfall und Wertewandel, durch Enthemmung und Hass in sogenannten sozialen Medien, durch Zunahme von manipulativer Meinungssteuerung und Einflussnahme mittels Fakes, durch außer Kontrolle geratene elektronische Bespitzelung (NSA) und zunehmende Cyberkriminalität, durch mediale Verführung und Werbung in den Massenmedien zu immer größerer Konsumsteigerung, durch eine wachsende Einkom-mensschere zwischen reich und arm und mit rapide steigendem Anteil von Armut und Arbeitslosigkeit: Dies alles sickert bzw. drängt in unsere Lebenssphären ein. Es verändert das gegenseitige Vertrauen, verstärkt Ich-Bezogenheit, verursacht Orientierungslosigkeit und sprengt soziale Kohärenz.

Diese rasanten Veränderungsprozesse und gewaltigen strukturellen Umbrüche, die viele bisherige Lebenssinne, also zahlreiches, bisheriges sinnvolles Leben massiv beeinflussen, einschränken oder in Frage stellen, sind seit längerem ein gesellschaftliches Dauerthema, das kontrovers diskutiert wird, um dessen Interpretationen und Deutungshoheit in der Multioptionsgesellschaft jedoch heftig gerungen wird. In diesem zuweilen abgehobenen Ringen führen die Intransparenz und das Unverständnis bezüglich der Wirkkräfte sowie die gefühlte Ohnmacht der Bürger, nichts ändern zu können und keine sinnvolle Lebensperspektive mehr zu haben, zu deren immer größeren Verunsicherungen, zu Verzweiflung, zu Zynismus, zu Verlust eigener Bedeutsamkeit, zu akuter oder chronischer Lebensunfähigkeit, zu Indifferenz, oft zur Flucht in Drogen, zu Depression oder sogar zu Lebensverweigerung mit Suizid.

Diesem Ohnmachtsgefühl und hilflosen Ausgeliefertsein, diesem „Gespenst der Nutzlosigkeit" (Sennett 2007) steht jedoch in der von Super-Diversität und funktionaler Differenzierung geprägten westlichen Welt eine Fülle von konkurrierenden und komplementären Sinn-Konzepten und Sinnquellen als Angebote für Sinnstiftung und Sinnerleben gegenüber, deren Rezeption und lebenspraktische Anwendung allerdings von Faktoren wie Ressourcen, von Persönlichkeitseigenschaften, Familienstand, Herkunft, Begabung, Alter etc. abhängen und von daher recht unterschiedlicher Propagierung und Vermittlungsstützen bedürfen. So können Menschen je nach eigener Bedürfnislage und Lebenssituation ganz unterschiedliche Lebensbedingungen und Ziele als sinnstiftend oder als sinnlos erleben (vgl. Schnell 2016, 31), wie etwa die Rekrutierung von Jugendlichen in Europa als IS Terroristen zeigt, die ihr Leben hier als sinnlos erachten.

Zur nochmaligen Verdeutlichung: Leben selbst hat keinen intrinsischen Sinn, Sinn ist stets relativ, ist variabel, nie einer Situation oder Idee per se inhärent, sondern wird immer subjektiv aus Quellen erschlossen und eigener Zielorientierung und eigenem aktiven Handeln zugeschrieben. Personen verleihen ihrem Leben also einen Sinn, indem sie Quellen heranziehen, die für sie selbst bedeutsam sind, Orientierungen geben und aus denen sie Sinn schöpfen.

Nachdem Philosophen, andere Wissenschaftler und Religionsvertreter seit Jahrhunderten versucht haben, den Sinn des Lebens zu identifizieren und ihren Anhängern vorzugeben und dabei zu einer großen Anzahl sehr unterschiedlicher Aussagen und Ergebnissen gekommen sind (McCaffrey 2017), hat nun die moderne Psychologie mittels empirischer Forschung detaillierte und nachprüfbare Ergebnisse vorgelegt: Es gibt keine universellen oder einmaligen Lebenssinn sondern nur den Sinn, den jeder einzelne Mensch seinem Leben gibt.

Breit angelegte empirische Forschungen auf dem Feld der Persönlichkeits- und der Differentiellen Psychologie zu Lebensbedeutung und Lebenssinn haben 26 Quellen in 5 übergeordneten Dimensionen identifiziert (Lebe, Schnell & Becker 2007), aus denen Menschen Sinn für ein sinnvolles Leben schöpfen. Dies sind:

Vertikale Selbst-Transzendenz	Horizontale Selbst-Transzendenz	Selbst-verwirklichung	Ordnung	Wir- und Wohlgefühl
Explizite Religiosität (3)	*Soziales Engagement (6)*	Herausforderung	Tradition	*Gemeinschaft (10)*
Spiritualität	*Naturverbundenheit (8)*	Individualismus	Bodenständigkeit	Spaß
	Selbsterkenntnis	Macht	Moral	Liebe
	Gesundheit	*Entwicklung (5)*	Vernunft	Wellness
	Generativität (1)	Leistung		*Fürsorge (2)*
		Freiheit		*Bewusstes Erleben (7)*
		Wissen		*Harmonie (4)*
		Kreativität (9)		

(Die stärksten Prädikatoren für Sinnerfüllung habe ich in der Tabelle in der Rangfolge 1-10 kursiv gekennzeichnet.)

Eigene kurze Befragungen in den Jahren 2017 und 2018 im internationalen Freundeskreis in Deutschland, Griechenland, Spanien und Portugal (N=21) zu Vorstellungen sinnvollen Lebens und zu Sinnquellen ergaben folgendes Ergebnis: *an erster Stelle stand Gesundheit (11), gefolgt von sozialem Engagement/aktiver Gestaltung des eigenen und des gesellschaftlichen Lebens (8), soziale und materielle Sicherheit und ein zufriedenstellender und sicherer Beruf (5), Freiheit und Frieden (4), Familie und Zuhause (4), gefolgt von Liebe und Eintracht (3), dann von Bildung, Freunden und Kindern, von Gebrauchtwerden (2) und zuletzt von Angstfreiheit, Partnerschaft, Selbstverwirklichung, Mobilität (1).*

3. Sinnfindung - Überlegungen, Voraussetzungen, Beispiele, Hinweise

Wie kommen wir zu einem sinnvollen Leben in unserer Welt, die derzeit aus den Fugen zu geraten droht? Was ist zu tun, welche Bedingungen sind dafür erforderlich, welche Inhalte können Sinn vermitteln? Dazu gibt es verschiedene Antworten aus unterschiedlichen Perspektiven, die jedoch in etlichen Aspekten übereinstimmen. Ich habe im Folgenden einige subjektiv ausgewählt, die meines Erachtens nach richtungsweisend und allgemeingültig sein können.

Sinn ist im Alltagsleben meist kein Thema und wird nicht hinterfragt, doch in belastenden Lebensphasen taucht die Frage nach dem Sinn im eigenen Leben wohl bei jedem Menschen auf, der dann sein Leben berührende, betreffende Ereignisse und die Sinnhaftigkeit eigenen Handelns darin kritisch in Frage stellt und dabei eine Art Selbstexploration vornimmt: Deshalb sind Sinnfragen für Hessel (2011) auch die Grundlagen von Empörung und Engagement, aus denen dann bewusste Konsequenzen/ Sinnfindungen hervorgehen können.

Ryff und Singer (1998) machen deutlich, dass sinnvolles Leben durch „invested and committed living" möglich ist, das heißt, sich einer Sache, die einem Leben Bedeutung geben kann, zu widmen, zu verpflichten, und sie konsequent umzusetzen. Das bedeutet, dass dieser Entscheidung ein bewusster, ein reflektierter Akt, eine geistige Auseinandersetzung vorausgehen muss, die Eigeninitiative verlangt. Viktor Frankl, der Begründer der Logotherapie, der 3.Wiener Schule der Psychotherapie, spricht in diesem Zusammenhang von einem „Willen zum Sinn", der jedem Menschen aufgrund seiner geistigen Dimension, seiner inneren Freiheit zur Wahl grundsätzlich eigen und aufspürbar ist. "Wer ein Warum zu leben hat, erträgt fast jedes Wie" – auf der Basis dieser Maxime erforschte Frankl, wie Sinnerfüllung auch angesichts schwerer Schicksalsschläge möglich ist und Menschen in die Lage versetzt, in Krisenzeiten seelisch heil zu bleiben. „Ein

Warum – das ist ein Lebensinhalt; und das Wie – das waren jene Lebensumstände, die das Lagerleben so schwierig machten, dass es eben nur im Hinblick auf ein Warum überhaupt tragbar wurde" (Frankl 2017).

Weitere Bedingungen für eigene Sinnfindung und für sinnvolles Leben sind die schon genannte persönliche Freiheit als Freiheit der Andersdenkenden und die Freiheit für eine eigene Wahl und Selbstbestimmung, die schon erwähnten 4 unverzichtbaren Kriterien: *Kohärenz, Bedeutsamkeit, Orientierung, soziale Zugehörigkeit;* des weiteren das Gefühl des *Gebrauchtwerdens,* sowie *gegenseitiger Respekt, Anerkennung und Bestätigung,* denn wir sind auf Gedeih und Verderb auf Kommunikation und Bestätigung angewiesen: „In allen Gesellschaftsschichten bestätigen Menschen einander (…) in ihren menschlichen Eigenschaften und Fähigkeiten, und eine Gesellschaft kann in dem Maße menschlich genannt werden, in dem ihre Mitglieder einander bestätigen" (Buber 1957, 102).

Mögliche Inhaltsfelder, in denen sinnvolles Leben zu finden ist, sind neben den zuvor in den Forschungsergebnissen erwähnten die Familie, die Arbeit, der Beruf und die Liebe; „Sinn erhält das Leben einzig durch die Liebe: das heißt: Je mehr wir zu lieben und uns hinzugeben fähig sind, desto sinnvoller wird unser Leben (Hesse 2008, 7). Weitere Sinnquellen bieten religiöse Institutionen (Orden), die Mitarbeit in NGOs und in Caritativen Organisationen (e.g. medecins sans frontières), besonders auch die ehrenamtliche, nicht finanziell vergütete Arbeit), wobei belegt ist, dass das Sinnerleben von ehrenamtlich Tätigen höher ist als das von Menschen ohne Ehrenamt (Hoof & Schnell 2009). Zudem eröffnen sich ganz viele, völlig neue Sinnquellen als Antwort auf Klimawandel und Ressourcenraubbau, wie etwa ein Engagement und Mittun in sehr progressiven Aktivitäten und neuen Lebensformen, die am Gemeinwohl orientiert sind, wie zum Beispiel *Tauschbörsen, Urban gardening oder Food-Coops* u. v. a. m.

Je stärker Aufgaben und Tätigkeiten als bedeutsam, sinnstiftend und sinner-füllend erfahren werden, desto größer ist die Wahrscheinlichkeit einer seelisch-geistig-körperlichen Gesundheit. Etliche Studien an der University of Rochester haben belegt: Sinnerfüllung korreliert positiv mit subjektiver Lebensqualität und objektiver Lebensdauer (vgl. Hill & Turiano 2014 und Schnell 2016, 114). Dass Sinnerfüllung eine motivierende Gesundheits-, Lebens- und Stressbewältigungskraft besitzt, hat auch Antonovsky in seinen Forschungen zur Salutogenese bereits 1979 nachgewiesen.

Als mögliche Leitlinie für Sinnfindung gebe ich Ihnen abschließend noch 4 Maximen an die Hand, die der kanadische klinische Psychologe Paul Wong als Extrakt aus seinen Forschungsergebnissen zu sinnvollem Leben aufgestellt hat:

1. Sie müssen sich einen angemessenen Vorsatz oder ein wichtiges Lebensziel wählen. 2. Sie müssen ein ausreichendes Verständnis dafür haben, wer Sie sind, was das Leben von Ihnen erwartet und wie Sie eine wichtige Rolle im Leben spielen können. 3. Sie und Sie allein sind dafür verantwortlich, zu entscheiden, welche Art von Leben Sie leben möchten und was ein wichtiges und lohnendes Lebensziel darstellt. 4. Sie werden nur dann ein tiefes Gefühl von Bedeutung und Zufriedenheit haben, wenn Sie Ihre Verantwortung für die Selbstbestimmung wahrgenommen und ein lebenswertes Ziel aktiv verfolgt haben (Wong 1998, 140).

Allerdings muss mit aller Deutlichkeit darauf hingewiesen werden, dass gerade die in den Eingangsfotos gezeigten bedürftigen Personen und Gruppen (Abgehängte, Ausgestoßene, Globalisierungsverlierer, etc.) und auch Menschen mit Behinderung besonderer personeller, finanzieller und institutioneller Unterstützung bei der Suche nach ihrem sinnvollen Leben bedürfen, um die sie bedrückenden Folgen von Globalisierung und Individualisierung der Lebensstile sozial abzupuffern und ihnen neue Orientierungen zu vermitteln.

Und wenn Sie es etwas lustiger und schlichter haben möchten, finden Sie in Monty Python's sketch comedy Film 'The Meaning of Life,' (1983) eine humorvolle Maxime: Am Ende des Films wird einer Person, die von Michael Palin gespielt wird, ein Umschlag mit dem Titel "Sinn des Lebens" ausgehändigt, den er öffnet und dem Publikum vorliest: *"Nun, das ist nichts Besonderes. Ähm, versuche nett zu den Menschen zu sein, vermeide es, Fett zu essen, lese ab und zu ein gutes Buch, geh hin und versuche, in Frieden und Harmonie mit Menschen aller Glaubensrichtungen und Nationen zusammenzuleben."*

Schlussbemerkungen

Sollten Sie selbst noch auf der Suche nach einem neuen oder weiteren Sinn für Ihr eigenes Leben sein, möchte ich Ihnen zum Schluss dafür 2 Anregungen mit auf den Weg geben, die ich bei Tatjana Schnell (2016) gefunden habe und für sehr kreativ und hilfreich halte:

- Führen Sie eine Woche lang ein *Sinntagebuch*, notieren Sie Ihre Tätigkeiten und reflektieren Sie am Wochenende sinnvolles und sinnleeres Tun;
- oder: Stellen Sie sich *Ihr Leben als Buch* vor, teilen Sie es in Kapitel ein und betiteln Sie diese (2016,149).

Zum Schluss biete ich Ihnen noch einige ausgewählte Zitate zum Nachdenken an:

- Der einzige Sinn des Lebens ist es, der Menschheit zu dienen. (Leo Tolstoi)
- In unserem Leben gibt es eine einzige Farbe, wie auf einer Künstlerpalette, die den Sinn von Leben und Kunst vermittelt. Es ist die Farbe der Liebe. (Marc Chagall)
- Das Leben ist ohne Sinn. Sie geben ihm den Sinn. (Joseph Campbell)
- Der Sinn des Lebens unterscheidet sich von Mensch zu Mensch, von Tag zu Tag und von Stunde zu Stunde. Entscheidend ist also nicht der Sinn des Lebens im Allgemeinen, sondern der spezifische Sinn des Lebens eines Menschen zu einem bestimmten Zeitpunkt (Viktor E. Frankl).

References

Buber, M. (1977): Distance and Relations. Psychiatry, 20, 1957.

Field, P. (2015): How to Live a More Meaningful Life (Huff Post), https://www.huffingtonpost.com/peter-field/more-meaningful-life_b_8118754.html.

Frankl, V. E. (2017): Wer ein Warum zu Leben hat: Lebenssinn und Resilienz.

Frankl, V. E. (2015, 18): Der Mensch vor der Frage nach dem Sinn.

Hesse, H. (2008): H. Hesse in einem Brief vom 16. Juni 1956 an M. Wedel, abgedruckt in: Hermann Hesse: Lieben, das ist Glück. Gedanken aus seinen Werken und Briefen. Liebe, Glück, Humor und Musik, zus. gestellt von V. Michels, Frankfurt am Main, S. 7.

Hessel, St. (2011): Tanz mit dem Jahrhundert. Berlin.

Hill, Patrick L.; Turiano, Nicholas A. (2014): Purpose in Life as a Predictor of Mortality Across Adulthood. In: Psychological Science, Vol 25, Issue 7. http://journals.sagepub.com/doi/abs/10.1177/0956797614531799.

Hoof, M.; Schnell, T. (2009): Sinnvolles Engagement. Zur Sinnfindung im Kontext der Freiwilligenarbeit. Weg zum Menschen, 61, 405-422.

Mayer, S.; Scheibler C.; Schmitt S.; Schöckel, A.-K. (o.J.): Ein sinnvolles Leben! Fallstudien. https://tinyurl.com/y2aaj89f.

McCaffrey, R. (2017): What is the meaning of life? Best to make up your own mind... https://tinyurl.com/y6bect6r.

Monty Python's 'The Meaning of Life. United International Pictures. British Board of Film Classification. 26 April 1983. Retrieved 21 July 2013.

Ryff und Singer (1998) (from case studies).

Schnell, T. (2016): Psychologie des Lebenssinns. Berlin/Heidelberg.

Schiffkoff, G. (1991): philosophisches Wörterbuch. Stuttgart.

Sennett, R. (2007): Die Kultur des neuen Kapitalismus. 67-103.

Berlin.

Smith, E. E. (2017): The Power of Meaning. Crown.

Steingart, G. (2016): Weltbeben. Leben im Zeitalter der Über
forderung. München.

Suttie, J. (2017): The Four Keys to a Meaningful Life. https://
tinyurl.com/y69poa6p.

Wong, P. T. P. (1998): Implicit theories of meaningful life and
the development of the Personal Meaning Profile
(PMP), in: P. T. P. Wong, & P. Fry (Eds.): The
human quest for meaning: A handbook of psychologi
cal research and clinical applications (pp. 111-140). Mah
wah, NJ: Erlbaum.

https://en.wikipedia.org/wiki/Meaning_of_life.

Meaningful Life in Old Age
Critical Thoughts on the „Active Ageing" Agenda

Jürgen Wolf

Old age and the demographic development

Talking about old age means to talk about the demographic development, i.e., older people as a growing population group which challenges society and policy. At the same time we talk about the individual experiences of growing old. Meaningful life in old age depends on both aspects: demography sets the framework conditions for experiencing life in old age. Thus, I am going to discuss the demographic development towards an „ageing society", have a look at the role of the family in the lives of older people, and then turn to changing old age images and approaches to deal with it, especially the concept of „active ageing" which has become predominant during the last years. My main topic does not concern the nature of ageing and ageing experiences but it deals with the way old age is viewed and discussed in public and the social sciences, especially in social gerontology.

Demography

While the demographic realities of most of the European countries can be characterized by longer lives, low fertility and inward migration, there is another picture to be drawn in others. Population levels are projected to increase for most of the Western Central European states, whereas in most of the eastern, post-communist countries like Ukraine, the number of inhabitants has decreased and still is projected to fall.

These decreases take place despite the fact that life expectancy is increasing but still below the central European average, though. In 2018, life expectancy at birth was 71.8 years in Ukraine (men 66, women 76 years), in the EU 81.6 years (men 78.9, women 76 years), in the EU 81.6 years (men 78.9, women 84.2) and 79,4 years world-wide in total. Population decrease takes place because of low fertility rates (1.46 children per woman) and migration, with negative net migration (cf. United Nations 2018).

Figure 1: Total population in Ukraine

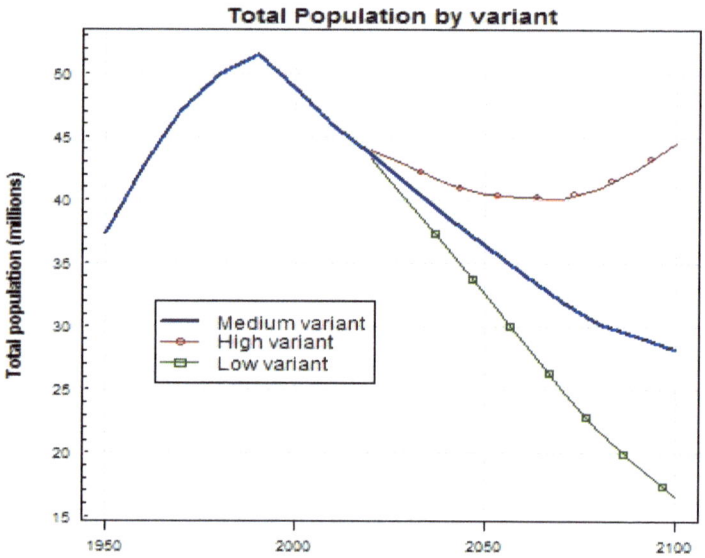

(Source: https://population.un.org/wpp/Graphs/DemographicPro-files/)

The world-wide development of our near future has been prospected by the United Nations, the World Health Organization (WHO) and others as globally ageing but divided into regions of the earth with an enormous diversity concerning economic conditions. Rather affluent countries are characterized by high life expectancy, only moderate population growth or even shrinking populations. Less affluent countries have to deal with ageing populations, too, but relatively high fertility rates and lower life

Figure 2: Natural population growth

Natural Population Growth of Ukraine

(Source: https://upload.wikimedia.org/wikipedia/commons/0/0f/
Natural_Population_Growth_of_Ukraine.PNG)

expectancy at the same time. Whereas Europe in general has an ageing but stable population, the eastern European states are confronted with shrinking populations, especially among the young, and growing proportions of older people. Ukraine can be seen as a special case somewhere in-between. This development will need special attention because it coincides with the fact that Ukraine as well as other eastern European countries has lower income levels, greater deprivation, lower life satisfaction, poorer health and less satisfactory housing than the central European countries, and especially is „increasing age associated with poorer quality of life and a lower rating of subjective well-being" (cf. Anderson et al 2009, 61).

While age in general has only limited effect on the level of life satisfaction, there is a marked divide between age groups. Differences exist in terms of optimism about the future. These results, which are especially true for people in the former communist countries, point into the direction that we have to consider the difference between ageing- and cohort-effects very carefully. The future perspectives are very different between younger and older cohorts and it may be very hard for the old to maintain biographical continuity from the former society in which they spent most of their lives and still have their biographical roots, to the new one. The elderly are of course a part of the society as a whole. But considering the gap between generations, the rich and the poor, and the tensions arising from it, it may result in new social conflicts, including a generational conflict which could lead to new risks of social exclusion for older people and others who could not find their place during the transition to market economies. From this point of view, the Elderly are a group at special risk. They are particularly vulnerable because only few are included in the labour market but most of them depend on welfare state provisions, i.e., the pension system. Main challenges for the Elderly will derive from the development of their economic, social, and cultural conditions.

Elder care and the family

Throughout Europe, the family is the main resource of elder care. The welfare state addresses older people predominantly but remain reliant on support networks, first of all the family, which serves as a „hidden welfare state" (Waerness 1978) beneath the level of state regulation. At the same time, there is a high prevalence of widow-hood among people aged 65 and over. A common family-based strategy to cope with such problems of support for the elderly is living in multigenerational households. In the Ukraine, there is a remarkable situation of older people living in „datcha"-based com-munities. This is particularly true for low-income households and may be seen as a way to ease economic strain.

Families, on the other hand, need support to manage the social and financial demands of elder care and child care. Considering the low income level and the high level of inequalities in eastern countries we can prospect a scenario which partly has become true already (Neuhaus & Weidner 2009). Younger women from poorer countries move to wealthier countries where they find jobs as private caregivers financed by the public care insurance or by the care receivers privately. But this behaviour, which is economically rational, may result individually in a deteriorated situation for the remaining elders in their home countries. They would experience a lack of support and an increase of social inequalities and deprivation in this scenario. An amazing case of such a development has already been reported for the situation of Albania. A massive rural out-migration since the 1990's has left behind older people and disrupted the multi-generational social and kinship systems. Without having any family members in their everyday lives, those elders feel like „orphan pensioners" who are disposed to a loss of self-respect and social appreciation (King & Vullnetari 2006). Such developments would be a serious challenge for countermeasures particularly on the community-based local level of newly designed social support systems and result in worsening the quality of life of the elderly.

Images of old age – The „active ageing" agenda

A different picture can be found if we take a look at mainstream gerontological approaches, political programmes, and the media (cf., e.g., Caprara et al. 2013; Walker 2010). Here, we witness a shift of the images of old age. We look at descriptions and pictures of a broad range of well-off, cheerful, leisure-oriented older people with lots of activities, engagements, and commitments. They reflect the shift from negative and deficit-oriented views of old age to an emphasis on activity, competence, and productivity. The Elderly are viewed in general as consumers as well as latent resources of productive engagement and commitment which have to be „activated". One of the instruments to measure the amount of activities is the „Active Ageing Index" (AAI) of the United Nations Economic Commission for Europe (UNECE) which provides rankings of the activating capacity of EU-countries.

Figure 3: Active-Ageing-Index Website

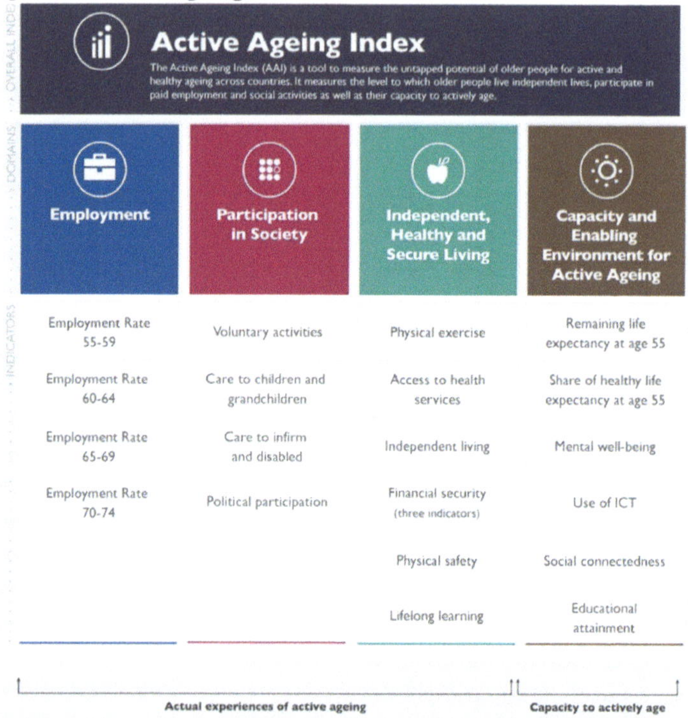

(Source: https://statswiki.unece.org/display/AAI/Active+Ageing+Index+Home)

Measures auf the „Active Ageing Index" are
- Employment
- Participation in society
- Independent, healthy and secure living
- Capacity and enabling environment for active ageing.

These measures go parallel to everyday activities of older people which are in the focus of social gerontologists and social politicians. In terms of gerontological theory it looks like „activity theory" has overcome the notion of „disengagement" as characteristic feature of old age. However, this change of perspective goes hand in hand with criticisms of an „overprovision" of elderly people, which in turn may cause new discriminating effects. The increasing emphasis on „successful" and „active ageing", as well as the resources and competences of elderly people in public is a process which contains similar contradictions. They rather do not show the unfavourable dark side of ageing for others who are not lucky enough to fit into these images. The Canadian gerontologist Stephen Katz pointed out that such activity-oriented approaches and studies based on these approaches show middle-class normative standards which are reflecting blind spots of gerontological research for social inequalities and most likely for intercultural differences: „Activity studies are often moored to traditional moral virtues; sex, drinking, and gambling, for example, are rarely registered. Indeed, what many activity checklists indicate as appropriate, normal, and healthy activities for older individuals are those which coincide with middle-class moral and family-oriented conventions. Most neglected are the activities of people who resist normalizing activity practices and inflexible scheduling" (Katz 2000: 144).

There is no doubt that activity is much valued by all ages but its meaning changes over time. One example is the changing involvement in social relations and social networks. It is a well-known fact that both are getting smaller in higher ages. American psychologist Laura Carstensen interpreted those empirical findings as a differentiated process with changing attitudes and motivations. According to her, network engagements are shrinking mainly in terms of quantitative dimensions rather than of qualitative ones. She explained this process in her „socio-emotional selectivity theory". As people get older, they achieve a shifting time perspective of their future, limited in length and less flexible when compared to younger adults. According to the theory, this shifting time-perspective contributes to the „positivity effect" where older adults regard positive events more significantly than negative events. A change in motivation or goal-orientation is suggested to accompany the shift in time-perspective. That is, younger adults focus on goals related to knowledge acquisition, like attending educational programmes, and older adults focus on goals related to emotion regulation in the sense of, for example, concentrating on meaningful social relations rather than a big amount of contacts and networks (cf. (Carstensen et al. 1999).

Figure 4: Socio-emotional Selectivity

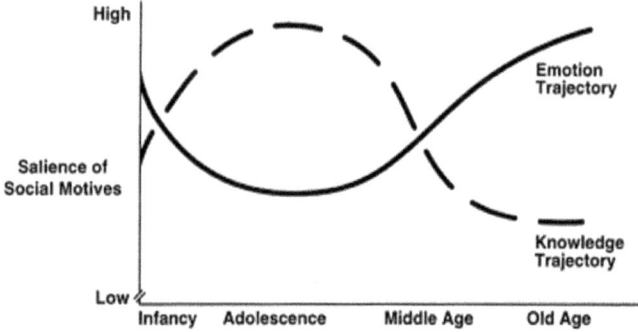

(Source: Carstensen et al. 1999)

Another change in activity patterns which may lead to an understanding of meaningful life in old age has been focused by Lars Tornstam's theory of gerotranscendence (cf., first, Tornstam 1989). He particularly pays attention to the old-old who use to prefer rather invisible, inner activities and concentrate their relationships on only the closest persons who in turn assume an increasingly important role. Tornstam reflects on the fact that old age is a stage of life like others with a crucial difference: it doesn't end, like the others, with the transition to a subsequent stage but with death – and this very fact may serve as a source of meaning in later life because it gives space to facilitate a growing need for transcendence in old age (cf. also the article by Wolfgang Heckmann in this volume).

Cultural gerontology takes such age specific differences and developments of the meaning of activities into account. It acknowledges them as „activities of resistance" (Katz 2000: 127) against the impositions of economic, health-related, leisure-oriented, and even sexual performance. Instead of promoting general activity patterns, gerontologists should listen to the people, encourage and support them by finding „diverse new ways of life that mobilize the true resources of time – tradition, wisdom, narrative, memory, change, generation, leadership – against the constraints imposed on them by a postmodern life-course regime and its stifling posthuman codes of functionality". (Katz & Marshall 2003: 13) There is lot of evidence that meaningful life in old age could rely on such factors – wherever you live.

Figure 5: Interviewing older Ukrainians

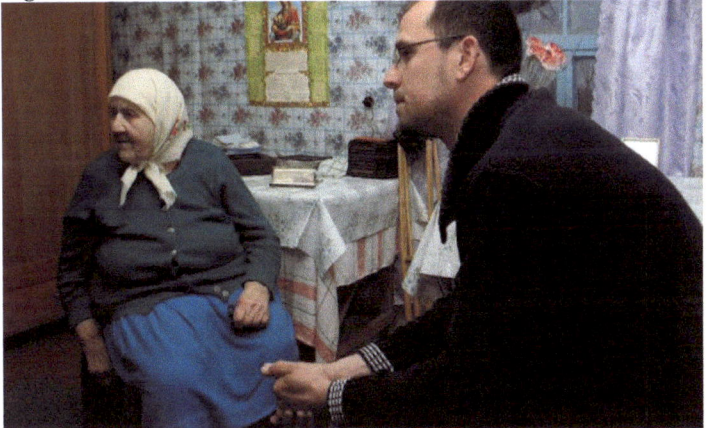

(Source: private)

An Ukrainian example

In the year 2012 Natalya Mosol published a contribution to a book on social inclusion in which she focused on older people in the Ukraine. She concluded her paper with the notion that „mostly people of this group are excluded and even 'socially eliminated'." (Mosol 2012: 121) She identified growing poverty and inequality, a lack of medical and social services and other serious problems which are imposed on elderly people more than on other groups. This diagnosis built the starting point for a study project which we conducted in Ukraine.

Let me conclude the question of meaningful life in old age by referring to the experiences we made during this project some years ago. In 2012, 10 Master's students from our university and a colleague of mine went to Ukraine for the first time – to the rural region of Perejaslaw Chmelnitzky, following an invitation from the local University. We expected to learn about the lives of older people in a country with heavy economic and social changes and living conditions of older people which are characterized by a low level of economic and social-political provisions. The students talked to the elders and listened to stories of their daily lives, their biographical past and future perspectives. Generally speaking, Natalya Mosol's diagnosis has proofed to be true for these people. But despite this fact, a common topic in almost every interview was surprising for us. It shed a light on a totally different aspect of the subjective experiences of getting older: our interviewees put an emphasis on the pursuit of happiness and told us stories which illustrated moments in which they experienced the feeling of happiness.

For a visitor from an affluent Western society, it was amazing to listen to stories of happiness instead of the obstacles of a difficult everyday life. Many stories dealt with the fact that children and other relatives moved to other places, some of them far away. On this background the researchers were told a striking definition of happiness. As one woman stated: „Happiness means the invention of the mobile phone". For a German speaking person, this phrase reflects the dual meaning of the German term „Glück" which has a two-fold meaning of the terms „luck" and „happiness". The invention of the mobile phone is experienced as the lucky condition of the possibility to experience happiness. The interviewees emphasize the fact that they can stay in touch with their relatives abroad by using this technology. It makes them happy in some way and thus may serve as a puzzle-piece of growing old in a self-determined way of a meaningful old age. In the future, new generations of older people in Ukraine will face new challenges. Will these elders remain a nearly invisible but self-confident group of „datcha"-citizens as whom they are viewed nowadays? What we can learn from this small example, maybe, is the need to listen to the people, to carefully try to understand their views and their perspectives to achieve a meaningful life in their own way.

References

Anderson, R.; Mikulič, B.; Vermeylen, G.; Lyly-Yrjanainen, M. & Zigante, V. (2009): Second European Quality of Life Survey – Overview. Luxembourg: Office for Official Publications of the European Communities.

Caprara M.; Molina M Á.; Schettini R.; Santacreu M.; Orosa T.; Mendoza-Núñez V M.; Rojas M. & Fernández-Balles teros R. (2013): Active Aging Promotion: Results from the Vital Aging Program. Current Gerontology and Geriatrics Research 2013: 1-14.

Carstensen, L. L.; Isaacowitz, D. M.; Charles S. T. (1999): Taking time seriously: A theory of socioemotional selectivity. American Psychologist. 54 (3): 165-181.

Katz, S. (2000): Busy bodies: activity, aging, and the management of everyday life. J. of Aging Studies 14: 135-152.

Katz, S. & B. Marshall (2003): New sex for old: lifestyle, consumerism, and the ethics of aging well. Journal of Aging Studies 17: 3-16.

King, R. & Vullnetari, J. (2006): Orphan pensioners and migrating grandparents: the impact of mass migration on old er people in rural Albania. Ageing & Society 26: 783-816.

Mosol, N. (2012): Social Support of Eldely People in Ukraine. In Neves, T., W. Bloemers, D. Johnstone, A. Magalhães, L. Cutleiro (Eds.), Education and Researchj on Social

Inclusion in Europe: Taking Stock of an Experience. Porto: 129-136.

Neuhaus, A.; Isfort, M. & Weidner, F. (2009): Situation und Bedarfe von Familien mit mittel- und osteuropäischen Haushaltshilfen. Köln.

Tornstam, L. (1989): Gero-transcendence: A reformulation of the disengagement theory. Aging, Vol. 1: 55-63.

Walker, A. (2010): The Emergence and Application of Active Aging in Europe. In: G. Naegele (Ed.), Soziale Lebenslaufpolitik, Wiesbaden: 585-601.

UNECE (2019): https://tinyurl.com/y3ommltg (Accessed on 15 February 2019).

United Nations (2017): Department of Economic and Social Affairs, Population Division (2017). World Population Prospects: The 2017 Revision, Online Demographic Profiles. (https://tinyurl.com/yd848k66, Accessed on 15 February 2019).

United Nations (2018): 2018 World Population Review. (https://tinyurl.com/y573j322, Accessed on 15 February 2019)

Waerness, K. (1978): The invisible welfare state. Women's work at home. Acta Sociologica, Supplement 1978.

Wikimedia (2013): https://tinyurl.com/y38bnohj (Accessed on 15 February 2019).

Особистісне становлення студентів соціономічних професій

Olena Chuiko

Проблема пошуку сенсів життя одвічна; віднаходження його подібне вичерпуванню води із колодязя; намагання філософів, антропологів, психологів, теологів відповісти на нього часто заводить в глухий кут і тоді, єдине, що може спасти у цій ситуації фраза нашого сучасника, психолога Володимира Петровича Зінченка: «Взагалі абсолютний сенс (сенс життя) важко вербалізувати, і про нього в пристойній компанії говорити не прийнято».

Але ми спробуємо. І я хочу розпочати свою доповідь, звернувши вашу увагу на 4 світлини, це світлини наших молодих сучасників, хлопців - українців, вік яких коливається від 21 до 25 років, які, як на мене, дуже рано віднайшли свої сенси і цілі в житті. Для мене їхні життєві історії – це підтвердження вислову Віктора Франкла «Смисл не є суб'єктивним, людина не придумує його, а знаходить у світі в об'єктивній дійсності».

Олександр Плеханов, 23 роки, студент 5 курсу Київського національного університету будівництва і архітектури. Герой Небесної Сотні (звання Героя України і орден Золотої Зірки (було присвоєно посмертно)). Загинув на Майдані. Свій сенс життя вбачав у відстоюванні ідей гідності і свободи українців.

Олег «Бандера», 22 роки доброволець. У зоні АТО перебував з липня 2014 року по серпень 2016 року (фактично 2 роки). Брав участь у визволенні населених пунктів Попасна, Лисичанськ, Піски, Опитне, у найгарячішій точці - Донецькому аеропортові 1.5 місяці. Сенс життя – захист держави Україна від російського агресора.

Владислав Малащенко, 21 рік, власник соціального підприємства, першим в Україні відкрив пекарню для людей з ментальною інвалідністю. Сенс життя – зламати стереотипи про неспроможність людей з інвалідністю, переконати про прав цих людей на незалежне і гідне життя.

Дмитро Ламза, 25 років, наймолодший директор школи (м. Київ, спеціалізована школа №210). Має три освіти. Виборов конкурс на посаду директора школи. Сенс життя - кардинально змінити освітній процес не лише у школі (що він фактично вже зробив), а й у всій державі.

Повторюю, ці молоді люди віднайшли свої сенси життя у досить молодому віці. Що слугувало причиною цього? Випадкові обставини, умови життя, кризові події, внутрішні інтенції й прагнення до самореалізація – кожен випадок унікальний. Але, я не випадково обрала цих молодих людей ще й тому, що їхній вік фактично співпадає з віком наших студентів.

Ці паралелі я провожу ще й тому, що студенти, яких ми навчаємо отримують професію, яка є смислоутворювальною по своїй суті. Стати психологом, чи стати соціальним працівником, соціальним педагогом – це не просто отримати диплом і зайняти робоче місце. Характер професійних задач в сфері соціономічних професій вирізняється нелінійністю, нестандартизованістю, пролонгованістю у часі. Кожного разу клієнтський запит – це унікальна ситуація –сплетіння причин і обставин, емоцій і розуму, закономірностей і випадковостей. Стати психологом – означає стати особистісно зрілою людиною, оскільки надавати смислову, емоційну чи екзистенційну підтримку людині або спільноті у важких чи кризових ситуаціях, здатна лише людина за умов розвитку особистісних структур вищого порядку.

Прийняте рішення у галузі соціономічних професій не може бути спонтанним, інтуїтивним, невідрефлексованим, в інакшому випадку воно стає об'єктивованим обмеженням, що перешкоджає вирішенню поставлених професійних завдань. Так, властивий юнацькому віку максималізм, впертість, спонтанність, амбіційність (або як часто кажуть психологи – непрацьованість особистісна) можуть ставати або ж гальмівним бар'єром у вирішенні професійних задач, або й взагалі доводити неспроможність у професії.

Звідси постає питання – чи можливе становлення зрілості в стінах університету, оскільки особистісна зрілість підпорядковується загальним законам онтогенетичного розвитку, а формування параметрів особистісної зрілості проходить ряд етапів, в яких чергуються періоди сенситивні, критичні і стабілізаційні.

Й тому видається, що «прискорити» зрілість особистості неможливо, її настання є результатом життєвого досвіду, вершинним етапом дорослої людини на життєвому шляху, коли певні особистісні риси досягають свого «зрілого апогею» (Е.Еріксон, А.Маслоу, К.Роджерс, Г.Салливан), а до того моменту усі ці якості перебувають лише в інтенційному стані.

- Чи можливе становлення особистісної зрілості в стінах університету?
- Чи можливо «прискорити» зрілість особистості?
- Якою має бути освіта, яка «запустить» процес особистісної зрілості (технологія «зсуву вікових рамок»)

Для того щоб спростувати, чи підтвердити ці припущення було проведено дослідження серед студентів факультету з 1 по 6 курси.

Серед цікавих результатів, виявились наступні:
1. Найбільш вираженими є зміни в ціннісно-смисловій сфері студентства. Причому, якщо магістри оцінюють минуле (навчання в ун-ті) як цінність, де є місце продуктивній самореалізації себе і своїх можливостей, то у бакалаврів відбувається дезорієнтація у побудові життєвих цілей, певна втрата сенсів. Означений стан виникає з одного боку, через невпевненість у набутих компетенціях,

47

а з іншого через достатню неоднозначність статусу «бакалавра», який у суспільній свідомості асоціюється із незавершеною (неповноцінною) вищою освітою.

2. Цікавими є зміни в індивідуально-особистісній сфері. Серед домінантних характеристик особистості досить вираженими виявились екстровертовані риси поведінки: ініціативність, впевненість, орієнтація на соціальні контакти, прагнення збагачувати життєвий досвід і керуватися самостійно прийнятими рішеннями, бути незалежними і контролювати ситуацію. Динаміка загострення цих рис спостерігається з роками. Водночас, студентам притаманний дещо завищений рівень домагань і власних амбіцій, нездатність визнавати власні прорахунки в ситуації невдачі і адекватно сприймати критику на свою адресу, невміння управляти емоційним станом в ситуаціях «нелінійного» характеру, в яких звинувачення швидше приписується іншій стороні, ніж звернене на власне «Я».

В результаті було сформульовано припущення, що «невизрівання» особистісних структур у процесі навчання, призводить до професійної непідготовленості випускника факультету соціономічного фаху виконувати професійні задачі.

В результаті, було запропоновано авторську концепцію, яка пройшла апробацію, і впродовж 4 років упроваджується кафедрою — концепція становлення (або й навіть вирощування) особистісної зрілості суб'єкта професійної діяльності.

Її особливості.

Ці відмінності зафіксовані в таблиці. Для порівняння ми взяли відомі концепції психологів –гуманістів і виокремили чотири важливих індикатори.

1. Генеза становлення.

Поняття «особистісної зрілості» знаменує досягнення людиною вершинного етапу розвитку (яке яскраво представлене в теоріях психологів гуманістичного напряму) і становлення якої відбувається у контексті життєвого шляху. Особистісна зрілість суб'єкта професійної діяльності проходить своє становлення у професійній діяльності, в яку включається індивід, і завдяки чому починають складатися базові психологічні структури, спрямовані на розв'язання специфічних професійних задач, які завжди пов'язані із необхідністю віднаходження сенсів (цілей, способів, екзистенцій) життя іншої людини.

2.   Головні індикатори особистісної зрілості

У відомих концепціях завше йдеться про перелік «зрілих» рис, вимір яких є річчю доволі суб'єктивною й важко вимірюваною (у Роджерса, наприклад, це «екзистенційний спосіб життя», Маслоу – «свіжість сприйняття», Олпорта – «широта границь Я») які, попри свого ціннісно-смислового значення, не мають відповідних процедур опису і вимірювання, й до того ж відносяться до різних рівнів властивостей людини).

В нашій концепції такими індикаторами є специфічні функціональні органи, особливі «здатності», які мають діяльнісну природу і доводять свою спроможність в ситуації розв'язання професійних задач.

1.   Характер становлення

На відміну від природнього або й стихійного характеру становлення зрілості особистості, в якому не можливо спрогнозувати причини і обставини, які вплинуть на її появу, ми

Говоримо про спеціальну заданість умов освітнього середовища, в якому особистісна зрілість проходить своє становлення.

2. Умови появи (за яких зрілість обов'язково матиме місце)

Екзистенційні психологи вказують, що для цього повинна

бути криза: особистісна, суспільна, але це обов'язково серйозний досвід переживань, який породжує смисли і робить ці смисли ціннісними.

За нашою концепцією, поява цих смислів у студентів можлива за умов включення їх у професійно-орієнтовані практики, які у «згорнутому» вигляді володіють квінтесенцією професійних смислів, цілей, цінностей і змістом майбутньої професійної діяльності.

За таких умов з'являються нові смислоутворювальні мотиви навчальної діяльності, в зв'язку з чим особистість надає діяльності особистісний сенс. Цей важливий ключовий момент діяльнісної теорії вітчизняної психології (автором якої є О.М.Леонтьєв) чудово ілюструють наші студенти. Як тільки вони включаються в професійно-орієнтовані практик, їхнє навчання набуває особистісних сенсів.

Ми виділяємо чотири типи професійно-орієнтованих практик: волонтерську, дослідницьку, проектну та організаційно-управлінську. Ці види професійно-орієнтованих практик розгортаються у «позанавчальному» форматі, тобто вони не внесені до навчального розкладу занять, але як особистісне включення в ці практики, так і результати - фіксуються у наукових роботах студентів: волонтерська, дослідницька, проектна у курсових роботах; організаційно-управлінська – у дипломних роботах (на IV і VI курсах).

Етап I – розробка технології проектування (за допомогою навчальних курсів „Основи соціальної інженерії")

Етап II – тренінг відкритого діалогу для формування об'єктивних комунікацій

Етап III – вивчення реального досвіду реалізації соціальних проектів у громадах

IV етап – створення команди, написання ідей проекту

V фаза – презентація ідей проекту на кафедрі

Стадія VI – проведення експертизи (Британська Рада)

VII – проект

VIII – звіт про проект (захист курсу) на кафедрі

Наостанок ми хочемо проілюструвати приклади, проектних практик, які у обов'язковому порядку виконуються нашими студентами 3 курсу.

Соціальні проекти студентів - 2017- 2018

1. Профілактика кібербулінгу серед підлітків у школі
2. Інклюзивна спортивна спільнота як засіб соціальної інтеграції студентів
3. Соціальні медіа як засіб інтеграції підлітків з вадами слуху
4. Читацький онлайн-квест як інструмент розвитку комунікативної компетентності підлітків
5. Створення студентської локальної спільноти

Назва: Online Reading-квест як інструмент для покращення комунікативної компетенції підлітків

Мета: створити навчальний онлайн-ігровий процес для підлітків

Очікувані результати:

1. Постійне співтовариство в соціальних мережах та регулярні онлайнові квести
2. Підлітки формують розуміння емоцій, їх причин і цінностей у житті людини, а також розрізнення емоцій, почуттів та настроїв, обговорюють його на форумах.
3. Підлітки розуміють різницю між сваркою та конфліктом, їх особливостями, знають різні стратегії конфлікту/суперечки та можуть використовувати це в реальному житті
4. Вводиться аналітична звичка читання

Назва: Ми разом_teens

Мета: побудова інклюзивного простору підлітків на принципі інверсивної суб'єктної інтеграції підлітків з порушенням слуху підліткового клубу „Відчуй".

Очікувані результати:

1. На основі проведених інтерактивних занять створення спільноти в соціальних медіа на тему спільних інтересів та дозвілля.
2. Проведення раз на місяць інклюзивних заходів для розширення сфери дозвілля підлітків та структурованого його проведення.
3. Налагодження комунікації в середині підліткового клубу.
4. Активізація громадської роботи .
5. Вироблення технологій соціально-педагогічної роботи з підлітками з порушенням слуху в рамках інтерактивних занять.
6. Впровадження тренінгового курсу для підлітків з порушенням слуху щодо формування суб'єктності та активної життєвої позиції.

Менеджери проекту: Мисник Марина, Владишевська Анна.
Назва: НУО „Грунтовно"
Мета: реформування вищої освітньої системи
Очікувані результати:

1. Студентська спільнота буде більш активною (більш особиста та спільна діяльність)
2. Розробка навчального простору, більш чутливого до сучасних потреб студентської спільноти
3. Зображення української вищої освіти буде більш привабливим. (Більше молодих людей з інших країн хотіли б навчатися в Україні)

Керівники проектів: Юрій Обач, Катерина Хоменко, Настя Якимова, Богдан Дяченко.
Інтеграція професійно-орієнтованих практик в освітній процес університету дозволяє:

- отримати досвід взаємодії із людьми різного соціального статусу, системи цінностей та інтересів;
- віднайти професійний і особистісний сенси;
- освоїти базові професійні компетенції (відповідальність за прийняті рішення, прогнозування, критичне мислення, емпатія тощо);
- освоїти етичні моделі (стандарти) професійної поведінки;
- отримати досвід презентації і самопрезентації на різних рівнях спільнот.

Personal Formation of the Students
of Socionomical Professions

Olena Chuiko

Oleksandr Plechanov, (1991-2014), fifth-year student of Kyiv National University of Construction and Architecture. Hero of Heavenly Hundred (Order of Hero of Ukraine with Order of Gold Star awarded posthumously).

Oleg Matsishin ("Bandera"), 22 years old, volunteer, was staying in ATO zone from July 2014 to August 2016. He was taking part in the liberation of settlements such as Popasna, Lysychansk, Pisky, Opytne and in the hotspot Donetsk airport (December 2015 – January 2016).

Vladyslav Malashchenko, 21 years old, owner of the social enterprise, first in Ukraine who opened a bakery for people with mental disabilities.

Dmytro Lamza, 25 years old, the youngest school's headmaster (Kyiv, specialized school № 210). Has 3 degrees. Fundamentally changed the educational process in school.

Sense is not subjective, human doesn't invent it, but finds it in the world of objective reality.

Viktor Frankl

- Is the formation of personal maturity possible at the university?
- Is it possible to "accelerate" maturity of the personality?
- What education should be that will "start" the process of personal maturity (technology of "shift of age frame")?

Results of the research

- The most pronounced changes in the value-notional sphere: past (studying at the university) is evaluated as value, where productive self-realization and realization of opportunities take place.
- Overestimated is the level of demand, projection, unrealistic plans, that are not backed up with personal responsibility for its realization.
- Tendency for self-acceptance; negative, critical and destructive attitude to oneself is changed to the possibility to perceive personal "I" from the positive point of view.
- Positive dynamics of the development of personal communicative sphere; basic professional communicative competencies are developed.
- Gradual increase of purposeful control over emotions and behavior; restraint, diplomacy, balancing is becoming pronounced.
- Inability to control emotional state in the situations of "nonlinear" character, where accusation is attributed to the other party, but not attributed to personal "I" ("professional egocentrism").
- Crisis of the bachelor (the loss of senses on the eve of the graduation from the university).

Concept of personal formation of the subject of professional activity		
	Theories of personal maturity	
Peculiarities	Maturity of personality (Rogers, Allport, Maslow)	Personal maturity of the subject of activity
Genesis of formation	Way of life	Professional activity
Main indicators	«Mature features» (freshness of perception)	Personal abilities
Character of formation	Spontaneous	Predetermined
Conditions of appearance	Crises, experience of feeling	Professionally-oriented practices

Professionally-oriented practices

Kind of students activity in socionomical specialties aimed at obtaining personal experience and experience living real situations and developments of professional ways of action in the future professions.

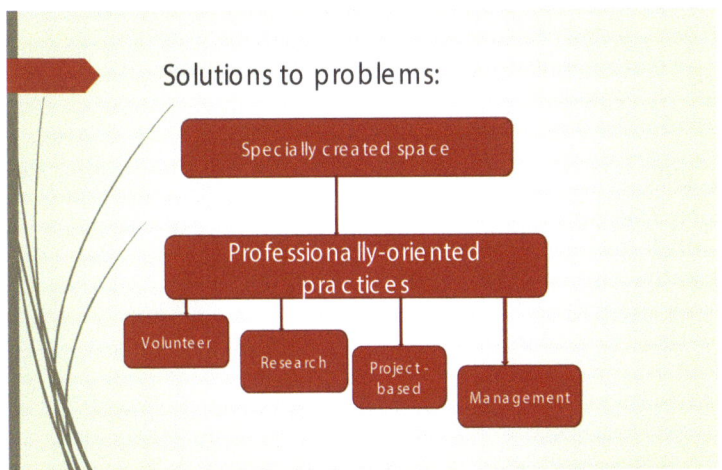

Solutions to problems:

Specially created space

Professionally-oriented practices

Volunteer

Research

Project-based

Management

Student engagement in project activities
- Stage I - development of design technology (through training courses Fundamentals of social engineering)
- Stage II - training open-minded dialogue to form unbiased Communications
- Stage III - study of the real experience of implementation of social projects in the communities
- IV stage - creation team, writing project ideas
- V phase - presentation of project ideas on the department
- Stage VI - passing expert evaluation (British Council)
- VII - the project
- VIII - report on the project (protection of course) at the Department

Social projects of students 2017-2018
1. Prevention of cyberbullying among adolescents in school
2. Inclusive sports community as a means of social integration of students
3. Social media as a tool for integrating adolescents with hearing impairments
4. Reader's online quest as a tool for the development of communicative competence of adolescents
5. Creating a Student Local Community

Name: Online Reading-quest as a tool for improving the communicative competence of adolescents
Aim: Create an educational online gameplay for teens
Expected results:

1. Permanent community in social networks and regular online quests
2. Adolescents have formed an understanding of emotions, their causes and values in human life, as well as the distinction of emotions, feelings and moods, discuss it on forums.
3. Adolescents understand difference between the quarrel and the conflict, their peculiarities, know different conflict/quarreling strategies and can use it in real life
4. An analytical habit of reading is introduced

Name: Ми разом_teens
Objective: create an inclusive space for Teens principle inversive integration of adolescents with hearing teen club "Відчуй".
Expected results:
1. Based on the interactive lessons creating community in social media on the topic of common interests and leisure.
2. Holding times per month inclusive of measures to expand the sphere of leisure of teenagers and structured the vote.
3. The establishment of communications in the middle of the teen club.
4. Revitalization of public works .
5. Development of technology of social-pedagogical work with adolescents with hearing impairment in the framework of interactive workshops.
6. Introduction training course for adolescents with hearing impairment in the formation of subjectivity and active life position.

Project managers: Marina Misnik, Vladyshevsky Anna.

Name: NGO "Gruntovno"
Objective: Higher educational environment reformation
Expected results:
1. Student's community will be more active (more personal and community activities)
2. Design of the educational space more sensitive to the modern needs of the student community

3. Image of Ukrainian higher education will be more attractive. (More young people from other countries would like to study in Ukraine

Project managers: Yurii Obach, Kateryna Khomenko, Nastya Yakimova, Bogdan Dyachenko.

Summary

Integration of project-based experience into the curriculum contributes to:
- a wide range of interactions with people of different social status, value systems and interests;
- independent experience of professional practices;
- mastering professional standards (including ethical) models and activities;
- personal development;
- presentation experience at various levels of communities.

The Meaning of Life and its Significance in a Difficult Period of Ukrainian Society

Lyudmyla Romanenkova

The ancient Egyptians believed that two things
are asked in front of the gates of paradise
1) Did you find joy in life?
2) And did your life bring joy to others?

The meaning of life is a spiritual problem that has to do with determining the ultimate goal of human existence. Meaning of life is one of the main worldview concepts, which is of great importance for the formation of the spiritual and moral image of the individual (Adler 1998).

The question of the meaning of life can also be understood as a subjective assessment of life, as a person's understanding of the content and direction of his life, his place in the world, as a problem of man's influence on the surrounding reality and setting personal goals in life (Adler 1931).

Understanding of the meaning of life are formed in the process of people's activities and depend on their social status, the content of the problems to be solved, the way of life, the world outlook, and the specific historical situation (Попов Б. Н. 1986).

Under favorable conditions a person can see the meaning of his life in achieving happiness and well-being; in a hostile environment of existence, life can lose its value and meaning.

The Austrian psychologist, psychiatrist and thinker Alfred Adler mentioned that from a medical point of view, all organs develop in the direction of the ultimate goal. The development of the soul is analogous to the development of organic life. Each person has a conception of purpose or an ideal necessary to achieve more than what is possible for him in the actual life situation. Without sensing the goal, the individual's activity would not make any sense (Adler 1930). At the same time, he adhered to the idea that the true meanings of life are common, those that other people can share and accept for themselves.

American psychologist Carl Rogers, one of the founders and leaders of humanistic psychology, speaks already of the purely individual character of the meanings of life. According to him, every individual exists in the constantly changing world of experiences, the center of which he is, and only a small part of the individual's personal world is experienced consciously (Rogers et al. 1967).

The Austrian psychiatrist, Victor Frankl, asserts that the understanding of the meaning of life differs not only from person to person, but also in different periods of the individual's life. The loss of the meaning of life - according to V. Frankl is a spiritual death (Frankl 2006).

A number of recent studies have shown that people who try to live with meaning often retain their liveliness in old age, are healthier mentally and even live longer than those whose goal is to receive pleasures (Helliwell et al. 2018).

The meaning of life is determined by specific historical conditions. Today in Ukraine there is a difficult political situation, which forces us to consider the question of our destiny and the meaning of life.

The person is formed through actions. I always looked at myself and identified myself with Russian nationality. The events of the last few years have made it possible to clearly define my belonging and form a rise in patriotism, not only for me, but for all my closest associates.

In February 2018, it was already four years since Russian President Vladimir Putin annexed the Crimea and helped the uprising in the industrial east of Ukraine. Since then, about 10,000 people have died, including 3,000 civilians and more than 1.7 million people have been displaced. Assistance agencies say that as a result of the ongoing fighting, about 4 million people were affected, and 3.8 million are in urgent need of assistance (Возняк 2015; Троян 2014).

Ukrainians have lost the understandable perspective and meaning of their further life, which is why anxiety, fatigue, pessimism and oppression are growing in the society.

As evidenced by numerous social surveys, there are fewer optimists in Ukraine. The society is growing aggression and anxiety. Now in mass sentiments pessimistic expectations concerning the nearest future of the country dominate. According to the latest data, more than half of the Ukrainians surveyed (53.9%) are „pessimistic" or „rather pessimistic" about the future of the country in a year. Only a third (35.7%) of respondents assesses the outlook for the development of the situation in one way or another optimistic. At the same time, there are quite a few (25%) radical citizens who believe that the goals of Euro Maidan were not achieved, and therefore – „a new revolution is needed" (Karber P. 2015).

Who and how helps people in such a difficult period of time? I would like present video to show you two women who together with many other citizens of Ukraine help at the zone where there is a war. Their names are Natalia and Svetlana. What they do is a heroism and the highest evidence of a very deep meaning in life they see – to serve other people for the better future of the country.

References

Alfred Adler (1998): Social Interest: Adler's Key to the Meaning of Life. Paperback – June 1, 1998. One World

Alfred Adler (1931): What Life Should Mean to You - Pp. 12-14. Edited by Alan Porter.

Alfred Adler (1930): Lecture given in Berlin, June 7, 1930. Originally published as „Der Sinn des Lebens" in the Internationale Zeitschrift für Individualpsychologie, Vol. IX, 1931, pages 161-171, 1931.

Antoine Arjakovsky (2014): Russie-Ukraine, de la guerre à la paix? – Paris: Parole et Silence. Український переклад: Розбрат України з Росією: стратегія виходу з піке

Frankl, V. E. (2006): Man's search for meaning. Boston

Frankl V. E. (1962): Man's search for meaning; an introduction to logotherapy. Boston.

Helliwell, J.; Layard, R. & Sachs, J. (2018): World Happiness Re port 2018, New York: Sustainable Development Solutions.

Karber. P. (2015): The Russian Military Forum: Russia's Hybrid War Campaign: Implications for Ukraine and Beyond, Center for Strategic and International Studies (CSIS), 10 березня.

Rajan Menon; Eugene B. Rumer (2015): Conflict in Ukraine. The Unwinding of the Post-Cold War Order.

Rogers, C. (1959): A theory of therapy, personality and interper sonal relationships as developed in the client-centered framework, in: S. Koch, Psychology (ed.): A study of a science. Vol. 3: Formulations of the person and the social context. New York.

Rogers, C. R.; Stevens, B.; Gendlin, E. T.; Shlien, J. M. & Van Dusen, W. (1967): Person to person: The problem of being human: A new trend in psychology. Lafayette, CA

Rogers, Carl (1980): A Way of Being. Boston: Houghton Mifflin.

Thomas D. Grant (2015): Aggression against Ukraine. Territory, Responsibility, and International Law. Palgrave Macmil lan.

Брехуненко В.; Ковальчук В.; Ковальчук М.; Корнієнко В. (2016): «Братня» навала. Війни Росії проти України XII XXI ст./За заг. ред. В. Брехуненка.

НАН України. Інститут української археографії та джерелознавства ім. М. С. Грушевського.(20196) К. - 248 с.

Возняк (2015): Геополітичні аспекти війни в Україні.(2015) - Львів: Незалежний культурологічний журнал «Ї»

Гай-Нижник П. П. Росія проти України (1990-2016 рр.): від політики шантажу і примусу до війни на поглинання та спроби знищення. (2017), К.: «МП Леся», 332 с.

Зеленкова, И. Л. (1988): Проблема смысла жизни: Опыт историко-этического исследования. Мн., 1988, 125 с.

Ирвин, Я. (1999): Экзистенциальная психотерапия. Часть IV. Бессмысленность. М.: Класс.

Леонтьев, Д. А. (1999): Психология смысла. М.: Смысл., С. 249-250.

Попов, Б. Н. (1986): Взаимосвязь категории счастья и смысла жизни. М.

Соловьёв, В. С (1996): Оправдание добра. М.: Республика, 1996. - С. 29-30, 189-193, 195-196.

Трубецкой Е. Н. (1918): Смысл жизни. М

Троян С.; Киридон А. Грузія (2008): Україна 2014 запаралелення російських стратегем. Зовнішні справи. 2014., № 8., С. 33-3.

Тимчук, Д; Карін, Юю; Машовець, К.; Гусаров, К. (2016): Вторжение в Украину. Хроника российской агрессии (рос.). Брайт Букс.

Social Representations of the Elderly in Romania - An Explanatory Study

Ion Dafinoiu and Irina Crumpei

"Social representations are an object of study, an object gifted with its own reality, unborrowed from other sciences, able therefore to constitute as a solid reference supporting the development of social psychology."
Adrian Neculau (1996)

Introduction

In the past years there has been a growing scientific interest in the topics of aging and old age caused by the global demographic changes that have been occurring in the structure of the population. The world population is aging as birth rate decreases and life expectancy increases worldwide (United Nations, 2001, 2007; WHO, 2002). The United Nations (2007) report that 21% of the Europeans were over 60 years old in 2007 making Europe the continent with the highest percent of elderly people in the world. Until 2050 it is estimated that one third of Europe's population will be over 60. Romania makes no exception and is already confronted with the economic and social consequences of the process of demographic aging.

In this global context the topic of aging becomes more and more socially relevant. Since 1930 life expectancy increased with almost two decades. The generations born at that time grew up with very different perceptions about old age, aging and elderly people. Understanding people beliefs about important social concepts is the first step in defining and implementing action and change. Social representations theory offers the needed platform to investigate shared views and beliefs about relevant social topics (Moscovici, 1976).

In the present study we try to observe Romanian beliefs about elderly people using a social representations approach. We discuss the specific Romanian context with its transition from communism to capitalism, dealing with the economic crisis. All these particular details affect people lives and beliefs.

Romanian aging population

The past century brought several social, economic and political changes that contributed to the current crisis. The industrialization, the urbanization, the transition from communism to capitalism, the economic crisis, have gradually altered the value scale. Emigration elevated, the birth rate decreased, life expectancy prolonged. We witness a declining percentage of the young population, aged 0-14 years, from 23.7% (in 1990) to 15.0% (in 2012) and a rising percentage of the elderly one, aged 65 years or over, from 10.3% (in 1990) to 15.0% (in 2012). The adult population, aged 15-64 years, has seen a constant rise from 66% (in 1990) to 70% (in 2012). For the first time over the last four decades, on January 1st, 2012, the weight of the young population was equal to the one of the elderly population (15%). In the last years we notice the tendency for a greater rise in the number of the "elder" elderly (from 0.8207 million in 1990 to 1.2 million in 2012), compared to the "younger" elder subgroup (from 1.4 million in 1990 to 1.8 million in 2012). From the total of 822.4 thousand persons, which represents the rise of the elderly population in the 1990-2012 period, over 60.4% pertains to the age group of 75 years or over. In 2012, "the longevous ", the population segment aged 85 years or over, represented 8% of the population aged 65 years or over, following an ascending line compared to 1990 (5.1%) (Institutul National de Statistica, 2012).

The number of economically active elderly persons (aged 65 years or was) was, in 2011, of 388 thousands, which represents 3.9% of the active persons total and 12.2% of the total population in the same age category. The economically inactive elderly persons (aged 65 years or over) formed 87.8% of the total number of the persons in this age category. The elderly population (aged 65 years or more) is less affected by poverty, the rate level being slightly inferior to the population average (14.1% in 2011) (Institutul National de Statistica, 2012).

The poverty rate among the elderly has considerably dropped in the 2008-2011 period, with almost 12 percentage points in 2011 compared to 2008. Nevertheless, in this age group, the differences are very significant, as the elderly women are much more affected by poverty than men. Thus, the poverty rate associated with women was of 17.7% in 2011, and that for men of only 8.7%. In the case of the single elderly: one in three persons in this age group is under the incidence of this risk. From the extended family that offered its members stability and safety, we turned to the family that gives its members' independence a key role. This mostly affects elderly people. Formerly, their place was in the family, nowadays they are more and more confronted with isolation, abandonment and institutionalization.

Social representations of the elderly people

Studies investigating people's beliefs about aging and old age report similar results in spite respondents' different nationalities and cultural backgrounds (Monchietti et al, 2000; Magnabosco-Martins et al, 2009; Gaymard, 2006; Gastaldi & Contarello, 2006). Differences are subtle and they often appear even in the same culture depending on age, gender or socio-economic groups. Beliefs focus on advantages and disadvantages of growing old describing physical and psychological changes. Regarding age there seems to be a pattern across different cultures. Younger people have a more negative view of old age which becomes more positive and concrete as they grow older. Wisdom is the quality often reminded along with numerous negative elements as illness, loneliness and death (Gastaldi & Contarello, 2006; Gaymard, 2006; Wachelke & Lins, 2008). Women seem to be more worried about the physical and aesthetic decline and loss of loved ones (Veloz et al, 1999). However, men seem to report more negative global views on getting old, while women focus more on the serene, careless life (Gastaldi & Contarello, 2006). Gender differences in social representations about aging might vary more culturally as specific patterns are difficult to define.

Wisdom and other related terms as experience are among the few positive elements reported as core ideas in the social representation of aging. They are usually accompanied by more negative terms as illness or dependency (Moliner & Vidal, 2003; Gaymard, 2006). Yet, older people are more positive and tend to differentiate a lot more between being old and feeling old (Beyene et al, 2002). Being old implies physical debilitating conditions and depending on others for basic needs while feeling old is a psychological state described as depression and loss of hope. An important concern for them is loneliness and abandonment at an older age and they emphasise the importance of family emotional support above other forms of support from their family (Beyene et al, 2002).

Cavanaugh (1997) suggests how relative age has become by reminding how 40 was considered already old age in the beginning of the nineteenth century. Nowadays 40 is still called young age and 65 is the end of middle age. Even if patterns can be identified in social representations across different cultures, differences do exist and people beliefs and values are constantly shifting.

The present study aims to explore the preliminary content of the social representations of the elderly persons. We expect results showing the complexity of the Romanian social context with patterns both similar and distinctive to previous studies. The collected data should be used to further explore the topic on a larger, representative group. Our hypothesis was that the central content of the representations is similar to the results reported previously by other studies in which old age is usually associated with negative concepts. However, some of the negative concepts will be related to the features of the Romanian socio-economic context. In other words, we expect that the content which is likely to be situated at the core of the representation is mainly built of negative concepts: loneliness, lack of money for daily expenses, fear of not getting needed care in case of health issues, lack of leisure activities, the need of supplementary, under qualified work for extra income and the distrust in government institutions that should help. Furthermore, it was expected that elderly women will be perceived as more vulnerable and categorized in a more negative way compared to elderly men.

Method

Sample

A total of 76 participants were surveyed, aged 19 to 82 with an average of 44 years old, 26 males and 50 females. They were from both rural and urban areas in the Moldavian region in Romania. 13 had elementary studies, 40 average and 23 superior.

Measures and Procedure

To explore the social representation of the elderly we used two different methods: the associative map (Abric, 1994) in order to explore the content and the elements which are candidates for centrality and the inductive method of the ambiguous scenario (Moliner, 1993) in order to verify the representational core.

The associative map, described by Abric (1994) starts with the free association instruction. The participant is asked to produce words associated to a stimulus word, or phrase. Secondly, the participant is instructed to produce a second set of terms associated to couples of words consisting of the original stimulus word and words produced in the first phase. Then, each of the triads is associated with a new word. Thus a complex network of elements is created, expressing the content and the structure of the representation.

The ambiguous scenario technique (Moliner, 1993) is meant to verify the core of the social representation. Firstly, the participant describes the object of interest. The purpose is to already acquire an idea of the social representation. Secondly, an ambiguous description of the object is created. The description is not clearly related to the object of interest and is presented to the participants stating two opposing conclusions: it is and it is not describing the object. Finally the participant is asked if the object described in the scenario presents the features considered essential for the object of interest. Depending on the choices made the items are central or peripheral.

All participants were presented with a Verbal Associative Test (Appendix 2). They were asked to write 5 words that first came to their minds when hearing the phrase "elderly person". Afterwards they were asked to write three words that came to mind for each of the five words previously written when associated with the phrase "elderly person". In the end we would have for each person 5 first degree associated terms and 15 second degree associated terms.

To further examine social representations, all participants were presented with an ambiguous scenario describing a person like any other in Romania worrying about being able to pay the due expenses for the apartment he/she lives in, with no optimistic perspective for the future and not being able to count on children's help (Appendix 1). Participants were divided into four experimental conditions. For the first two conditions participants were told the person described was an old lady or an old man. For the other two conditions participants were told the person described wasn't an old lady, respectively an old man. All participants were asked to assess the probability of the person being faced with each of six problems: loneliness, lack of money for daily expenses, fear of not getting needed care in case of health issues, lack of leisure activities, the need of supplementary, under qualified work for extra income and the distrust in government institutions that should help. Answers were reported on a five point Likert scale where 1 meant surely not and 5 surely yes. The ambiguous scenario was pre-tested on 50 people to make sure it wasn't necessarily describing an elderly person. Chi square test results showed no significant difference (p > .001) between the frequency of people thinking the scenario was about an elderly person and those who didn't.

Participants took part voluntarily in the study. They were informed the study investigated social representations. All participants were guaranteed confidentiality and anonymity.

Results

We computed the total score for the Ambiguous Scenario method by adding up the scores for the 6 dimensions (Cronbach's Alpha = .60). We conducted a one-way ANOVA test with follow-up Bonferroni comparisons to observe differences in assessment across the four experimental conditions. The analysis showed significant differences across the experimental conditions $F(3.72)=6.64$, p = .001.

Table 1. *Total probability ratings across different experimental conditions*

Experimental Condition			
1A. Elderly man	1B. Elderly woman	2A. Adult man	2B. Adult woman
17.50$_a$	25.40$_b$	21$_a$	21.20$_a$

Note. Judgments were made on a 5-point scale (1 = surely not, 5 = surely yes). Means that do not share subscripts differ at p < .05 in the Bonferroni difference comparison.

Note. Judgments were made on a 5-point scale (1 = surely not, 5 = surely yes). Means that do not share subscripts differ at p < .05 in the Bonferroni difference comparison.

Bonferroni post-hoc comparisons of the four groups indicate that the elderly women were perceived as significantly more probable to be confronted with the six issues compared to elderly men or adult men and women.

We conducted one-way ANOVA tests for each of the six dimensions. Assessments differed across the four conditions in four of the six dimensions: loneliness $F(3.72)=4.70$, p = .005, lack of money $F(3.72)=3.14$, p = .03, health care $F(3.72)=3.28$, p = .026 and extra under-qualified work $F(3.72)=4.02$, p = .011. There were no significant differences in lack of leisure activities $F(3.72)=.34$, p = .79 and distrust in government institutions $F(3.72)=1.43$, p = .23.

Table 2. *Detailed probability ratings across different experimental conditions*

Dimensions	Experimental Condition			
	1A. Elderly man	1B. Elderly woman	2A. Adult man	2B. Adult woman
Loneliness	2.50_a	4.1_b	3.11_{ab}	3.9_b
Lack of money	3.1_a	4.6_b	3.69_{ab}	3.85_{ab}
Health care	3.1_a	4.6_b	3.47_{ab}	3.35_a
Extra work	3_a	4.6_b	3.94_{ab}	3.45_{ab}

Note. Judgments were made on a 5-point scale (1 = surely not, 5 = surely yes). Means that do not share subscripts differ at p < .05 in the Bonferroni difference comparison.

Women, both adult and elderly were perceived to suffer significantly more from loneliness compared to elderly men. Elderly women are perceived as significantly more probable to lack money for daily expenses compared to elderly men. In consequence they also are more likely to need extra under-qualified work to complete their income compared to elderly men. Elderly women are perceived as more likely to have health care issues compared to elderly men and adult women.

We applied Independent Samples T Test to analyse the differences in the assessment of the gravity of issues based on gender. Women assess the severity of the issues described in the questionnaire (M = 22.40) as significantly greater compared to men (M = 18.80; t(74) = -3.64, p<0.001).

The Verbal Associative Test generated mostly negative associations for the phrase "elderly person". The first order associations with the highest frequency were: illness (45), helpless

(29), pensioner (28), grandparent (22), alone (20) and wise (12). Other first order associations were: worries, faith, nosy, suffering, picky, leisure etc. Second order association continued with mostly negative terms: abandoned, sadness, widow, poor, incapable, dept, pain. The only terms associated with positive ideas were grandparent (help, love, happiness) and wise (calm, advice, experience).

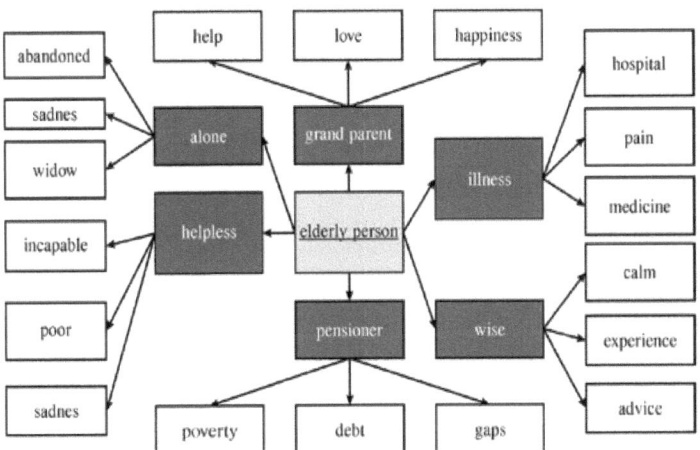

Discussions

The results provide some support for our hypothesis, are consistent with previous studies and are supported by the statistical data showing Romanian demographic situation. Elderly women were perceived as most vulnerable, being significantly more likely to suffer from loneliness, lack of money, health problems or need for extra work compared to elderly men or even adult men and women. Elderly women have the highest scores on all dimensions while elderly men have the lowest scores. These results are in agreement with the national statistical data reported by the National Institute of Statistics (2012). The elderly population is slightly less affected by poverty even if the differences in income are very important among people in this age group. Elderly women are twice as affected by poverty than men. International studies support these results showing that women, more than men, tend to be subjected to the negative biases associated with older age (Mcconatha et al, 2004). For example, women are considered "old" at a younger age even if they live longer than men.

We found no differences across the four experimental conditions for two of the dimensions: leisure time activities and confidence in government institutions. The ambiguous scenario described a person of uncertain age facing some financial difficulties. The responses recorded in our study suggest that people distrust government institutions regardless of their age. This is in line with a Special Eurobarometer report (2007) on European Social Reality which shows that 67% of Romanians don't trust any political institutions. Leisure time seems to be more linked to social possibilities than age group in Romanian perceptions.

Our results suggest that women assess the issues people are confronted with as being more serious. Previous studies show significant gender differences in the worry report of women and men, with women often showing more worry than men, intolerance to uncertainty and negative problem orientation (Robichaud et al, 2003).

Our associative map shows representation patterns similar to other studies on the same topic. The central core is likely to be formed of six elements: illness, helpless, pensioner, grandparent, alone and wise. However, our results indicate that only three of these six terms have negative connotations, confirming just partially our initial hypothesis. This can be explained by the small and unrepresentative group of participants. Previous research shows cultural differences in associations between aging and exclusion from social life. Italians show a stronger attachment to family and a better integration of their elders compared to Brazilians who perceive old age a lot more linked to social exclusion (Contarello et al, 2008; Wachelke & Contarello, 2010). Our first order associations show a double idea about social life suggested by the terms: grandparent and alone. It seems that the elderly persons can be part of the family as grandparents. The second order terms show that by offering help they can get "love" and "happiness" in return. Loneliness is a risk in the absence of grandchildren. Family relations for emotional support as alternative to loneliness in old age are among the most important ideas for both men and women regardless of cultural background (Beyene et al, 2002; Wachelke & Contarello, 2010). Among the concerns most reported by the elderly people are fear of loneliness and the prospect of living in nursing homes (Beyene et al, 2002). Romanian associations suggest a similar pattern as "loneliness" is linked to "abandonment", "widowhood" and "sadness". "Illness" and "helplessness" are also very often elements in elderly people social representations (Moliner & Vidal, 2003; Gaymard, 2006). They come to define being old as part of the physical decline (Beyene et al, 2002). "Wisdom" associated with "calm", "advice" and "experience" is also consistent with international perceptions of elderly persons (Gastaldi & Contarello, 2006; Gaymard, 2006; Wachelke & Lins., 2008). The only first order association that seems to be more cultural specific is "pensioner". The transition between active professional life and retirement can be very financially steep in Romania. Even if statistics show a smaller poverty rate among the elderly persons, the differences among the rich and the poor can be significant (Institutul National de Statistica, 2012). Desperate poverty cases among the elderly persons are very visible in mass media. Pensions' situation was strongly emphasized as both last year and next year are electoral years. This context can explain the high association between elderly persons and financial decline that appears to be stronger in Romanian perceptions than in other countries.

Conclusions

The study provided a preliminary view of the social representations of elderly people, with data collected from a small and unrepresentative sample from the north-eastern region of Romania. Results are largely consistent with patterns reported in previous studies on the same topic. Overall, the associations split between the physical and psychological changes. Illness and helplessness are elements associated to the physical decline, while wisdom, loneliness and grandparenthood are related to the psychosocial perception. Terms with negative connotations are part of the central core of the representation. In particular, the retirement associated with a low pension, debts and poverty seems to be an element more cultural specific in the associative map. The economic crisis and media emphasis on pensions between electoral years could explain this particular association.

We acknowledge some limitations of the current study. First, the small number of participants may impact the reliability of the representation. Analysis of variance results should also be interpreted with caution. Second, the unrepresentative group is another weakness limiting the generalizability of results. Third, the concepts that accompanied the ambiguous scenario were inferred from previous studies, most of them referring to different socio-economic settings.

Further studies, should use the data reported in this preliminary work to create scenarios better adapted to the Romanian context for a thorough exploration of the central content of the representation. Larger, better distributed samples are needed to provide results with higher reliability, representative for the Romanian population.

Note:

This study was first published in: Psihologia Sociala. 32(II), 185-196, edited by Alexandru Ioan Cuza University, Faculty of Psychology and Educational Sciences

References

Abric, J C. (2003). Méthodes d'études des représentations socia les. Paris.

Beyene, Y., Becker, G. & Mayen, N. (2002) Perception of aging and sense of well-being among Latino elderly Journal of Cross-Cultural Gerontology 17: 155–172.

Cavanaugh, J. C. (1997) Adult development and aging. Pacific Grove.

Contarello, A.; Bonetto, D.; Romaioli, D. & Wachelke, J. (2008). Invecchiamento e intercultura. In Incontro Tematico Associazione Italiana di Psicologia: Spazi Interculturali: Trame, Percorsi, Incontri. Roma: Università degli studi di Roma "La Sapienza".

Gastaldi, A. & Contarello, A. (2006). Una questione di età: rappresentazioni sociali dell'invecchiamento in giovani e an ziani. Ricerche di Psicologia, 20(4), 7-22.

Gaymard, S. (2006). The representation of old people: comparison between the professionals and students. Revue Internationale de Psychologie Sociale, 19(3-4), 69-91.

Magnabosco-Martins, C.R.; Camargo, B.V. & Biasus, F. (2009). Representações sociais do idoso e da velhice de diferentes faixas etárias. Universitas Psychologica, 8(3), 831-847.

McConatha, J.T., Hayta, V., Rieser-Danner, L., McConatha, D., & Polat, T.S. (2004). Turkish and U.S. attitudes toward ag ing. Educational Gerontology, 30 : 169-183.

Moliner, P. (1993). ISA : l'Induction par Scénario Ambigu. Une méthode pour l'étude des représentations sociales. Revue Internationale de Psychologie Sociale, 2 : 7-21.

Moliner, P. & Vidal, J. (2003). Stéréotype de la catégorie et noyau de la représentation sociale. Revue Internationale de Psychologie Sociale, 16(1), 157-176.

Monchietti A.; Cabaleiro, I.R.; Sànchez M. & Lombardo E. (2000). Representaciones de la vejez. Revista Latinoamericana de Psicologia, 32(3), 519-536.

Moscovici, S. (1976). La psychanalyse, son image et son public. Paris.

Neculau , A. (1996) Reprezentarile sociale – dezvoltari actuale. In A. Neculau (Ed), Psihologie sociala. Aspecte contemporane, Iasi : Polirom.

Institutul National de Statistica (2012) Raport - structura populatiei.

European Commission (2007) Special Eurobarometer 273 European Social Reality http://ec.europa.eu/public_opinion/archives/ebs/ebs_273_en.pdf.

Robichaud, M., Dugas, J. M., Conway, M. (2003) Gender differences in worry and associated cognitive-behavioral (17), 5: 501–516.

United Nations (2001). World population ageing: 1950-2050. New York: United Nations.

United Nations (2007). World population ageing. New York: United Nations.

Veloz, M.C.T.; Nascimento-Schulze, C.M. & Camargo, B.V. (1999). Representações sociais do envelhecimento. Psicologia Reflexão e Crítica, 12 (2), 479-501.

Wachelke, J.F.R. & Lins, S.L.B. (2008). Changing masks: a masking effect on young people's social representation on aging? Current Research in Social Psychology, 13(19), 232-242.

World Health Organisation (2002) Active Ageing. A Policy Framework http://whqlibdoc.who.int/hq/2002/WHO_NMH_NPH_02.8.pdf

Appendix 1

Ambiguous scenario:

Mr. (Mrs.) X is a person like many others in Romania over the last years. He/She lives in a privately owned apartment and worries about the possibility to pay all the living expenses in due time, while the economic situation of the country is not likely to provide hopes for the future. He/She can't even conceive receiving help from the children.

Experimental conditions

Mr. (Mrs.) X is (is not) an elderly person.

Please imagine this person's life and evaluate with grades from 1 - "definitely not" - to 5 - "definitely yes", the probability that he/she is confronted with the following issues:

Appendix 1

Ambiguous scenario:

Mr. (Mrs.) X is a person like many others in Romania over the last years. He/She lives in a privately owned apartment and worries about the possibility to pay all the living expenses in due time, while the economic situation of the country is not likely to provide hopes for the future. He/She can't even conceive receiving help from the children.

Experimental conditions

Mr. (Mrs.) X is (is not) an elderly person.

Please imagine this person's life and evaluate with grades from 1 - "definitely not" to 5 - "definitely yes", the probability that he/she is confronted with the following issues:

	1	2	3	4	5
Loneliness					
Lack of money to buy the requisites for everyday life					
The fear that, in case of illness, he/she won't receive the necessary medical care					
Lack of leisure activities					
The need to work overtime, as an unskilled worker, to compensate the revenues					
The feeling that the state institutions should provide help in resolving different issues that don't work properly					

Age :
Education : ❏ elementary, ❏ medium, ❏ higher
Gender : ❏ male ❏ female

Appendix 1

Ambiguous scenario:

Mr. (Mrs.) X is a person like many others in Romania over the last years. He/She lives in a privately owned apartment and worries about the possibility to pay all the living expenses in due time, while the economic situation of the country is not likely to provide hopes for the future. He/She can't even conceive receiving help from the children.

Experimental conditions

Mr. (Mrs.) X is (is not) an elderly person.

Please imagine this person's life and evaluate with grades from 1 – "definitely not" to 5 – "definitely yes", the probability that he/she is confronted with the following issues:

	1	2	3	4	5
Loneliness					
Lack of money to buy the requisites for everyday life					
The fear that, in case of illness, he/she won't receive the necessary medical care					
Lack of leisure activities					
The need to work overtime, as an unskilled worker, to compensate the revenues					
The feeling that the state institutions should provide help in resolving different issues that don't work properly					

Age :
Education : ☐ elementary, ☐ medium, ☐ higher
Gender : ☐ male, ☐ female
Provenance area : ☐ rural, ☐ urban

Appendix 2

Write five words that come to mind when you hear the phrase "elderly person":

X^1 ....
X^2 ....
X^3 ....
X^4 ....
X^5 ....

Now write three words that come to mind when you hear the phrase "elderly person – X^1
.... " :

A^1 ....
A^2 ....
Age: A^3 ....

Education: ☐ elementary, ☐ medium, ☐ higher

Gender: ☐ male, ☐ female

Provenance area: ☐ rural, ☐ urban

Was denken 90 meiner Freunde und Verwandten über ein sinnvolles Leben

Fritz-Helmut Wisch

Nachdem ich das Konferenzthema gelesen hatte, fragte ich mich: Wie kann ich als Emeritus von 75 Jahren etwas zu diesem beitragen, bzw. welche Antworten kann ich zu diesem Thema präsentieren, mit dem sich Philosophen und Denker seit Jahrhunderten – nicht nur in Europa – auseinandergesetzt haben.

Diese gaben im Verlauf der Geschichte Europas unterschiedlichste Antworten, auf die wir hier nicht eingehen können, vielmehr auf Internethinweise (z. B. Wikipedia) und andere verweisen.

Eine zentrale Antwort finden wir sowohl in der Bergpredigt als auch in der Goldenen Regel (lat. regula aurea; engl. golden rule): Liebe deinen Nächsten wie dich selbst (Markus 12, 29-31) – ist das vielleicht wichtigste Gebot von Jesus und wird gemeinhin mit dem Christentum gleich gesetzt. Das Gebot der Nächstenliebe stammt allerdings ursprünglich aus der hebräischen Bibel und findet sich in ähnlicher Form in allen Weltreligionen. Gleiches gilt übrigens für die Goldene Regel, einem alten und verbreiteten Grundsatz der praktischen Ethik: „Behandle andere so, wie du von ihnen behandelt werden willst." Oder negativ ausgedrückt: „Was du nicht willst, dass man dir tu, das füg auch keinem andern zu." Bevor ich Ihnen meine kleine Befragung vorstelle, möchte ich einleitend noch Teile aus der berühmten Rede des Friedensnobelpreisträgers Martin Luther Kings zitieren, die er vor knapp 55 Jahren, am 28. August 1963 vor mehr als 250.000 Menschen hielt und die unter dem Titel I Have a Dream in die Geschichte eingegangen ist.

Martin Luther King träumte unter anderem von Freiheit, Gleichheit und Brüderlichkeit. Liberté, égalité, fraternité waren ja bekanntlich die Ideale der Französischen Revolution. In deren

Folge wurde mit der Erklärung der Menschen- und Bürgerrechte (Déclaration des Droits de l'Homme et du Citoyen) von 1789 das Gottesgnadentum abgeschafft, und die Souveränität im Staat ging auf das Volk über. Seitdem gilt dieser Grundlagentext auch als Geburtsstunde der Demokratie.

So I say to you, my friends, that even though we must face the difficulties of today and tomorrow, I still have a dream. It is a dream deeply rooted in the American dream that one day this nation will rise up and live out the true meaning of its creed - we hold these truths to be self-evident, that all men are created equal.	Heute sage ich euch, meine Freunde, trotz der Schwierigkeiten von heute und morgen habe ich einen Traum. Es ist ein Traum, der tief verwurzelt ist in dem amerikanischen Traum. Ich habe einen Traum, dass eines Tages diese Nation sich erheben wird und der wahren Bedeutung ihres Credos gemäß leben wird: Wir halten diese Wahrheit für selbstverständlich, dass alle Menschen gleich erschaffen sind.
I have a dream that one day on the red hills of Georgia, sons of former slaves and sons of former slave-owners will be able to sit down together at the table of brotherhood.	Ich habe einen Traum, dass eines Tages auf den roten Hügeln von Georgia die Söhne früherer Sklaven und die Söhne früherer Sklavenhalter miteinander am Tisch der Brüderlichkeit sitzen können.
I have a dream that one day, even the state of Mississippi, a state sweltering with the heat of injustice, sweltering with the heat of oppression, will be transformed into an oasis of freedom and justice.	Ich habe einen Traum, dass sich eines Tages selbst der Staat Mississippi, ein Staat, der in der Hitze der Ungerechtigkeit und Unterdrückung verschmachtet, in eine Oase und Gerechtigkeit verwandelt.
I have a dream my four little children will one day live in a nation where they will not be judged by the color of their skin but by the content of their character. I have a dream today!	Ich habe einen Traum, dass meine vier kleinen Kinder eines Tages in einer Nation leben werden, in der man sie nicht nach ihrer Hautfarbe, sondern nach ihrem Charakter beurteilen wird. Ich habe einen Traum heute ...

Täglich werden wir überflutet mit Nachrichten von Kriegen, Krisen und Konflikten. Einen Perspektivwechsel empfiehlt der kürzlich verstorbene schwedische Wissenschaftler Rosling, der uns auf die schönen Seiten des Lebens aufmerksam machen möchte und darauf hinweist, zwischen all den Negativschlagzeilen auch mal das Positive zu sehen. Er hat gemeinsam mit seinem Sohn und dessen Frau ein Buch geschrieben, das Anfang April 2018 erschien: „Factfulness. Wie wir lernen, die Welt so zu sehen, wie sie wirklich ist", heißt es. Die Autoren belegen mit vielen Fakten, dass unsere häufig negative Wahrnehmung der Welt (alles wird immer schlimmer, früher war vieles besser) ein Trugbild ist. In Wahrheit wird die Welt immer besser, das belegen die Daten glasklar.

- In den vergangenen zwanzig Jahren hat sich der Anteil der Menschen, die in extremer Armut leben, fast halbiert.
- Während 1970 noch 28 Prozent aller Menschen Hunger litten, sind es heute nur noch 11 Prozent.
- Die Lebenserwartung hat sich seit Beginn des 19. Jahrhunderts mehr als verdoppelt.
- Fast 90 Prozent aller Menschen haben heute Zugang zu Wasser aus einer geschützten Quelle, 85 Prozent haben Zugang zu Strom.
- Die Kindersterblichkeit ist weltweit auf 4 Prozent gesunken.
- 86 Prozent aller Menschen können zumindest grundlegend lesen und schreiben.

In einem Aufsatz, den Rosling für die „Frankfurter Allgemeine Sonntagszeitung" geschrieben hat, beantwortet er die Frage, warum wir Menschen so oft denken, die Welt werde immer schlechter, folgendermaßen: „Das hat zum großen Teil mit unserem Instinkt der Negativität zu tun, unserer Neigung, das Schlechte aufmerksamer wahrzunehmen als das Gute. Hier kommen drei Dinge zusammen: eine unzutreffende Erinnerung an die Vergangenheit, eine selektive Berichterstattung durch Journalisten und politische Aktivisten sowie das Gefühl, dass es hartherzig oder gewissenlos wäre, von Verbesserungen zu sprechen, solange es immer noch schlimme Dinge gibt."

Zu ähnlichen Resultaten gelangt der Nobelpreisträger für Wirtschaft Angus Deaton, der unter anderem nachweist, wie das Durchschnittseinkommen in den USA zwischen 1970 und 2010 in allen Schichten gestiegen ist.

Kommen wir nun zu meinem eigentlichen kleinen Beitrag: Im Zusammenhang mit unserem Konferenzthema habe ich ca. 100 Personen aus meinem Verwandten-, Bekannten- und Freundeskreis gebeten, mir anhand eines Fragebogens ihre spontanen Einschätzungen zu den Bedingungen bzw. Voraussetzungen für ein sinnvolles Leben mitzuteilen. Einige kritische Anmerkungen meiner Freunde zu meiner Befragung möchte ich Ihnen nicht vorenthalten:

1. Pfarrer: kann und will den Fragebogen nicht beantworten, da zu wenige christliche Elemente erkennbar sind.
2. Professorin (verheiratet mit einer Frau): war aufgrund mangelnder Gendersensibilität nicht bereit zu antworten. Lieber Fritz …, aber… Freunde/Brüderlichkeit? Vielleicht eine geschlechtsneutrale Formulierung? (=Freundinnen bzw. Schwesterlichkeit)
3. Medizinerin: Hallo lieber Fritz, anbei die Antworten der Familie … bezüglich Deiner Befragung. Spannendes Thema, hat zu einigen Diskussionen bei uns geführt. Wir wünschen viel Erfolg und Freude bei der Reise und den Vorträgen. Liebe Grüße …
4. Lehrerin & Mediziner: Der Fragebogen hat heftige Diskussionen zwischen meinem Mann und mir ausgelöst. Ich möchte gerne zwischen Glauben und Religion trennen und habe mit dem Ehrenamt Probleme. Ehrenamtlich Tätige sind sehr wichtig, ich persönlich kann das nicht. Uns fehlt der Bereich Natur
5. Redaktionsleiter einer deutschen Zeitschrift: Die Bewertung

fällt uns nicht leicht. Du hast die Kriterien hervorragend herausgearbeitet.

6. Heimleiter (Anthroposoph): Spiritualität statt Religion, Grenzenloses Reisen = keine abgeschotteten Länder z. B. Nordkorea

Die Antworten auf meine Befragung zum sinnvollen Leben habe ich in einer Übersicht zusammengefasst, die ich im Folgenden kurz erläutern möchte. In dieser Zusammenfassung habe ich weder die Altersangaben noch die Geschlechtsunterschiede berücksichtigt, da die entsprechenden Unterschiede nicht relevant waren. Von den Angeschriebenen beantworteten 90 meine Fragen.

Wir sehen, dass die ersten 13 Bereiche (96%-76%) von den Befragten als sehr wichtig eingeschätzt werden. Diese sind: Friede, Freiheit, Gesundheit, Bildung, Ehrlichkeit, Menschlichkeit, Demokratie, Familie, Liebe & Nächstenliebe, Freunde & Brüderlichkeit, Verlässlichkeit, Toleranz und Arbeit.

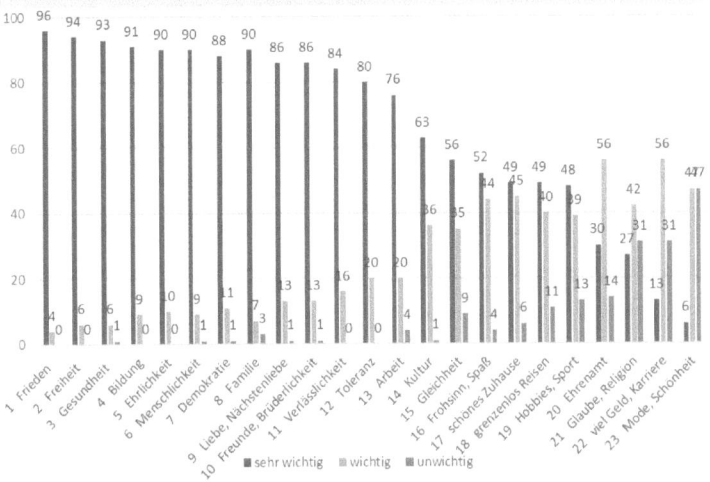

SINNVOLLES LEBEN BEDEUTET FÜR 90 PERSONEN MEINER VERWANDTEN UND FREUNDE
Angaben %

63 bis 48 Prozent sehen folgende Themenbereiche ebenfalls als sehr wichtig an. Diese sind: Kultur, Gleichheit, Frohsinn & Spaß, schönes Zuhause, grenzenloses Reisen, Hobbies & Sport. Für wichtig halten immerhin 56 Prozent die Komplexe Ehrenamt (Nr. 20) sowie viel Geld und Karriere (Nr. 22).

Eher unwichtig in Bezug auf sinnvolles Leben sind für die Befragten die Themen Glaube und Religion (Nr. 21), und zuletzt Mode und Schönheit (Nr. 23).

Nach diesen Ergebnissen unserer Befragung möchte ich Sie abschließend noch mit einer zukunftsrelevanten Untersuchung bekannt machen, welche von der Stiftung für Zukunftsfragen, Eine Initiative von BAT zu den Erwartungen für das Jahr 2030 (Forschung aktuell, 275, 38. Jg., 26.12.2017) veröffentlicht wurde. Wie stellen sich die Deutschen das Leben im Jahr 2030 vor? Diese Fragen standen im Fokus der neuesten Untersuchung der BAT-Stiftung für Zukunftsfragen. Sie befragte hierfür über 2.000 Bundesbürger ab 14 Jahren in persönlichen Interviews zu ihren Erwartungen für das Jahr 2030. Ein Kernergebnis lautet: Deutschland ist und bleibt in vielerlei Hinsicht das Land der Skeptiker und Pessimisten. So erwarten beispielsweise 84 Prozent der Befragten eine starke Zunahme der Kriminalität im Internet. Zur Angst vor Verbrechen meint der Leiter der Stiftung, Professor Dr. Ulrich Reinhardt: „Ob Angst vor Terroranschlägen oder Überfremdung, Einbrüchen oder dem Klimawandel – viele Bundesbürger haben das Gefühl, in unsicheren Zeiten zu leben. Parallel verlieren sie zunehmend das Vertrauen in Politik, Unternehmen und Medien. All diese Institutionen sind daher gefordert, mehr Sicherheit, Beständigkeit und Optimismus zu vermitteln sowie langfristige Lösungswege einzuschlagen.“

10 Erwartungen der Deutschen für 2030:

1. Die Kriminalität im Internet hat sehr stark zugenommen
2. Aus Sicherheitsgründen gibt es eine flächendeckende Videoüberwachung
3. Durch hohe Energiepreise ist die Warmmiete doppelt so

hoch wie die Kaltmiete

4. Die meisten Bürger blicken mit Zuversicht in die Zukunft
5. Der Klimawandel konnte dank technischer Entwicklungen gestoppt werden
6. Die Familie ist und bleibt das Wichtigste im Leben
7. Sonnen- und Windenergie erzeugen über die Hälfte der Energie
8. Service und Beratung sind wichtiger als ein günstiger Preis
9. Informelle Bildung[1] ist wichtiger als formale Bildung
10. Angehörige tragen finanzielle Verantwortung für Rente der Eltern/Großeltern

Sehr positiv stehen die Deutschen auch dem Thema Familie gegenüber. Die große Mehrheit (91%) stimmt der Aussage zu: „Familie ist 2030 das Wichtigste im Leben." Gerade in unruhigen Zeiten beweist sie sich als eine Konstante im Leben und erlebt in jeglicher Hinsicht eine Renaissance. Ebenso zeichnet sich auch ein Anstieg der Mehrgenerationenhaushalte ab, die einerseits finanziell notwendig und andererseits – gerade von der jungen Generation – auch gesucht, geschätzt und gewünscht werden.

Ein abschließendes Fazit von Reinhardt lautet: „Das Leben im Jahr 2030 wird in vielen Bereichen anders sein als heute. Die Ängste und Sorgen der Bevölkerung vor diesen Veränderungen müssen ernst genommen werden. Statt nur Antworten auf die Frage ‚Wie werden wir in Zukunft leben?' zu suchen, sollte sich zunächst darauf konzentriert werden, wie wir in Zukunft leben wollen. Denn ganz gleich, welche Möglichkeiten wir zukünftig haben, der Mensch mit all

---

1   Wer im Rahmen seines Hobbys, seines Ehrenamts oder in seinem Alltag außerhalb von Bildungsinstitutionen lernt, lernt „informell". Zum Beispiel: Menschen gehen einem Problem nach und versuchen, es zu lösen. Dabei lernen sie teils bewusst, teils unbewusst. Es wird in den jeweils bestehenden sozialen, familiären, kommunikativen oder auch Arbeitszusammenhängen gelernt. Kinder lernen am Computer (z. B. Wikipedia, FaceTime, WhatsApp…).

seinen Bedürfnissen muss stets im Mittelpunkt aller Veränderungen stehen, so dass das Leben auch in Zukunft lebenswert bleibt."

Literatur

Deaton, Angus (2017): Der große Ausbruch. Von Armut und Wohlstand der Nationen, Stuttgart.

Karliczek, Anja (2018): Wir sollten die Schulen umbauen. In: DIE ZEIT 2018, Nr. 14, S. 73.

Reinhardt, Ulrich (2017): Erwartungen für das Jahr 2030. In: Forschung aktuell, 275, 38. Jg., 26.12.2017.

Rosling, Hans (2018): Factfulness. Wie wir lernen, die Welt so zu sehen, wie sie wirklich ist. Berlin.

Smith, Zadine (2018): Romantische Liebe? Uninteressant! Fragen an das Leben. In: christmon 04.2018, S.48.

Що думають про сенс життя мої 90 друзів та родичів

Fritz-Helmut Wisch (Фриц-Хельмут Виш)

Після прочитання теми конференції, я запитав себе: як я можу, користуючись своїм життєвим досвідом 75-річної людини, внести свій вклад в це, і які відповіді можу дати з цієї теми, над якою працювали філософи і мислителі протягом сторіч і не тільки у Європі .

У ході європейської історії вони дали багато різних відповідей, про які ми не будемо говорити тут, бо у якості посилання на них можна використати інтернет-джерела, приміром, Вікіпедію.

Ключові відповіді ми знаходимо як у Нагірній проповіді, так і в «Золотому правилі» (Latin aurea, golden rule of English).

«Люби свого ближнього, як самого себе» (Марка 12: 29-31), мабуть, є найважливішою заповіддю Ісуса і загалом прирівнюється до християнства. Однак початок вона бере з єврейської Біблії і є у подібній формі у всіх світових релігіях.

Те ж саме стосується і Золотого Правила, старого і широко поширеного принципу практичної етики – «Ставтеся до інших так, як ви хочете, щоб вони ставилися до вас» або висловлювання з негативним забарвленням: «Не робіть іншим того, чого не бажаєте собі».

Перш ніж я ознайомлю вас з результатами мого маленького опитування, я хотів би процитувати частини знаменитої промови «У мене є мрія» лауреата Нобелівської премії миру Мартіна Лютера Кінга, яка прозвучала менш ніж 55 років тому, 28 серпня 1963 року, перед аудиторією в 250 000 людей.

Крім того, Мартін Лютер Кінг мріяв про свободу, рівність та братерство. Liberté, égalité, fraternité були, як відомо, ідеалами французької революції. У результаті Декларація про права людини та громадянські права (Déclaration des Droits de l'Homme et du Citoyen) від 1789 р. скасувала божественне право, а суверенітет у державі передавався людям. Текст, оголошений тоді, з тих самих пір вважається надзвичайно важливим для зародження демократії:

«Я говорю вам сьогодні, друзі мої, що, незважаючи на труднощі і розчарування, у мене є мрія. Це мрія, яка глибоко укоренилася в американській мрії. У мене є мрія, що настане день, коли наша нація повстане і доживе до істинного змісту свого девізу: «Ми вважаємо очевидним, що всі люди створені рівними».

У мене є мрія, що на червоних пагорбах Джорджії настане день, коли сини колишніх рабів і сини колишніх рабовласників зможуть сісти разом за столом братерства.

У мене є мрія, що настане день, коли навіть штат Міссісіпі, пустельний штат, що знемагає від напруження несправедливості і гноблення, буде перетворений в оазис свободи і справедливості.

У мене є мрія, що настане день, коли четверо моїх дітей житимуть у країні, де про неї судитимуть не за кольором їхньої шкіри, а за тим, що вони за люди. У мене є мрія сьогодні».

Кожен день нас засипають новинами про війни, кризи і конфлікти. Дослідник із Швеції Рослінг рекомендує змінити перспективу і звернути нашу увагу на позитивні сторони в житті, знаходячи їх навіть серед негативних заголовків на шпальтах газет.

Покійний вчений Ганс Рослінг написав книгу зі своїм сином і його дружиною, вона опублікована на початку квітня 2018 року «Сприйняття фактів. Як навчитись бачити світ таким, яким він є насправді». Автори доводять, що наше, часто негативне, сприйняття світу (все стало набагато гірше, раніше було набагато краще) хибне. Насправді, світ стає краще, що доводять наведені нижче дані

• За останні двадцять років частка людей, які живуть в

умовах крайньої бідності, зменшилася майже в двічи.

- Протягом 1970 року від голоду страждало 28 відсотків людей проти 11 відсотків сьогодні.
- Середня тривалість життя зросла більш ніж в двічі з початку 19-го століття.
- Майже 90 відсотків людей мають доступ до чистої питної води, 85 відсотків користуються електрикою.
- Дитяча смертність знизилася на 4 відсотки у всьому світі.
- 86 відсотків людей можуть читати і писати.

В ессе, яке написав Рослінг для «Frankfurter Allgemeine Sonntagszeitung», він відповідає на питання про те, чому ми, люди, так часто думаємо, що світ виглядає гіршим:

«Це пов'язано в значній мірі з нашим інстинктом негативу, нашою схильністю сприймати погане уважніше, ніж хороше. Ось три речі разом: неправильна пам'ять про минуле;часткове висвітлення реалій журналістами і політичними діячами у ЗМІ; рівно як і відчуття, що було б безсердечно і безсовісно говорите про те, що є покращення, доки так багато негативних явищ».

Аналогічні результати отримав нобелівський лауреат, економіст Ангус Дейтон, який доводить, що середній дохід у всіх сферах у США у проміжок між 1970-2010 роки збільшився.

Дозвольте тепер перейти до результатів мого дослідження:

У зв'язку з нашою темою конференції я попросив близько 100 моїх родичів, знайомих та друзів повідомити мене за допомогою анкети про їх спонтанні оцінки вимог та умов для змістовного життя.

Я запропонував своїм друзям:

Ви витратите близько 5 хвилин, будь ласка, подивіться на наступну таблицю, на якій в 23 стовпцях названі умови змістовного життя ... Поставте навпроти кожної з них помітку ... за шкалою від 0 = неважливо до 10 = дуже важливо) і надішліть мені ваші відповіді на імейл.

Я хотів би поділитися з вами деякими критичними зауваженнями моїх друзів щодо анкети.

1. Пастор не може і не буде відповідати на анкету, оскільки вбачає у ній занадто мало християнських цінностей.

2. Професорка (одружена із жінкою) не бажає відповідати через відсутність гендерної чутливості: Шановний Фріц ... але ... товариство / братерство? Можливо гендерно-нейтральне формулювання? (єдність подруг чи сестринство)

3. Ерготерапевтка: Шановний Фріц, Дякую за анкету. Однак я не хочу заповнювати це. Тема "життя, що має сенс" супроводжувала мене весь час, особливо на роботі. Як часто я обговорювала цю проблему з важко хворими людьми або навіть людьми, які страждають деменцією? Для мене "осмисленим" є те, що випливає з цього слова. Я відчуваю, дихаю тощо. Тут я не можу сказати, що через зовнішні обставини для мене відкривається сенс життя. Скільки людей через неврологічні захворювання вже не відчувають власного тіла? Це викликає тривогу і неспокій, почуття і відчуття через це важко класифікувати. Якщо після інсульту чоловік пояснює, що вночі він заснув мертвою рукою, де осмисленість? Ось чому я не можу нічого відповісти. Бажаю вам успіхів у своїх лекціях. Наприкінці лютого я також проведу лекцію в Ессені, зважаючи на те, що лекція в університеті Віттені-Гердеку пройшла успішно. З повагою . ... Лікарка: Привіт дорогий Фріц, щодо відповіді сім'ї ... щодо твого опитування. Захоплююча тема призвела до деяких дискусій між нами. Ми бажаємо тобі великого успіху та радості в дорозі та лекціях. Вітаю ...

5. Вчителька та лікар: Анкетування викликало гарячі дискусії між моїм чоловіком і мною. Я хотіла би розділити пріоритети між вірою і релігією і у мене виникла проблема із благодійністю. Благодійність дуже важлива, але я цього не

роблю. Нам не вистачає сфери «Природа».

6. Редактор одного з німецьких журналів: Нам нелегко дати оцінку. Ти дуже добре розробив критерії.

7. Завідувач дитячого будинку (антропософ): Духовність замість релігії, подорожі без кордонів= ніяких ізольованих країн, таких, як Північна Корея.

У контексті дослідження я нещодавно знайшов деякі надзвичайно розумні відповіді на питання про життя:

• Авторка і професорка творчого письма з Нью-Йоркського університету Заді Сміт відповіла на питання про кохання, багатство і радість:

Яка любов робить вас щасливою? Любов часто є нарцисичною за своєю суттю. Зрештою, люди просто лестять одна одній і хочуть бачити образ, який вони уявляють про себе, а інші підтверджують. Але це є таким захопливим, доки ви не одружилися. Звичайно, у тому, що Ісус у Біблії ніколи не був одруженим, є вагомі причини.

Про багатство: Бути багатим означає, що бути хорошим майже неможливо. Ця вимога прописана у Біблії, і Біблія має рацію: Легше верблюду пройти через вушко голки, ніж багатому потрапити в рай. Це одна з найреальніших речей, коли-небудь написаних.

Як щодо життя без гумору/веселощів? Я не знаю, як люди виживають без гумору. Англійські комедії можуть бути дуже близькі до трагедії — мені подобається одночасно плакати і сміятися.

• Новий федеральний міністр освіти Німеччини Аня Карлічек (Християнсько-демократичний союз) на питання: що означає для вас освіта? Навчання, з одного боку, є метою: людина потребує базової освіти, щоб брати участь у житті. З іншого боку, людина потребує освіти, щоб працювати за професією. Країні потрібна освіта для виживання в міжнародній конкуренції.

Я підсумував відповіді на моє опитування про життя, що має сенс, в короткому огляді, який я наведу нижче. У цьому підсумку я не враховував інформацію про вік чи гендерні відмінності, оскільки вони не були важливими.

Зі 100 респондентів 90 відповіли на мої запитання.

Ми бачимо, що перші 13 пунктів (96% - 76%) вважаються дуже важливими. До них відносяться: мир, свобода, здоров'я, освіта, чесніть, людство, демократія, сім'я, кохання і любов до ближнього, друзі і братерство, надійність, толерантність і робота.

63% - 48% вважають наступні теми дуже важливими. До них відносяться: культура, рівність, радість, гарна власна оселя, подорожі без кордонів, хоббі і спорт.

Пункти волонтерство (20) і багато грошей і кар'єра (22) отримали по 56%.

Швидше неважливі, з точкою зору змістовного життя для респондентів віра і релігія (21) та мода і краса (23).

Після результатів цього опитування, я хочу вас познайомити ще з інформацією, яку оприлюднив Фонд дослідження проблем майбутнього.

Прогнози на 2030 рік:

Як німці уявляють собі життя в 2030 році? Ці питання були в центрі уваги останнього опитування, проведеного Фондом дослідження проблем майбутнього. В опитуванні прийняло участь більш ніж 2000 осіб у віці від 14 років.

Одним із ключових висновків є те, що Німеччина була і залишатиметься країною скептиків та пессимістів за багатьма показниками. Наприклад, 84 відсотки респондентів очікують значного зростання злочинності в Інтернеті. Голова фонду, професор Ульріх Хайнхард: «Щодо страху терористичних актів або відчуження, зломів або зміни клімату – у багатьох німців є відчуття життя в смутні часи. У той же час вони все більше втрачають довіру до політики, бізнесу та засобів масової інформації. Тому всім цим інституціям пропонується забезпечити більшу безпеку, послідовність і оптимізм, а також шукати довгострокові рішення ".

Десять прогнозів щодо 2030 року

1. Злочинність в Інтернеті дуже зросте

2. З міркувань безпеки держава впровадить загальне відеоспостереження

3. Внаслідок високих цін на енергоносії, плата за комунальні послуги в опалювальний сезон зросте вдвічі.

4. Більшість громадян впевнені у майбутньому.

5. Зміна клімату буде зупинена завдяки технологічним досягненням

6. Сімейні цінності є і залишаться надзвичайно важливими.

7. Сонячна та вітрова енергія складуть більш, ніж половину енергересурсів.

8. Сервіс та консультації важливіші за низьку ціну

9. Неформальна освіта* важливіша ніж формальна освіта

10. Родичі несуть матеріальну відповідальність за пенсію батьків / дідусів та бабусь.

* Будь-хто, хто навчається за межами навчальних закладів заради хоббі, волонтерської роботи чи повсякденного життя, навчається "неформально". Наприклад: люди зіштовхуються із проблемою і намагаються її вирішити. Вони навчаються частково свідомо, частково несвідомо. Це явище існує в усіх соціальних, сімейних, комунікативних або навіть робочих контекстах. Діти навчаються за допомогою комп'ютера (наприклад, Вікіпедія, FaceTime, WhatsApp ...)

Німці також дуже позитивно ставляться до теми сім'ї. Більшість (91%) погоджується з твердженням: "Сім'я - це найважливіша річ у житті 2030 року". Особливо в неспокійні часи родина надає відчуття постійності в житті, сімейні цінності переживають своє відродження. Подібним чином, також спостерігається збільшення кількості родин, в яких кілька поколінь проживають під одним дахом, що, з одного боку, є вигідним, а з іншого боку – особливо для молодших поколінь – бажаним і цінним.

Як висновок, Рейнхард стверджує: "Життя 2030 року буде відрізнятися від того, яким воно є сьогодні, у багатьох сферах. Страхи і занепокоєння населення про ці зміни треба сприймати серйозно. Замість того, щоб просто шукати відповіді на питання "Як ми будемо жити в майбутньому?", ми повинні спочатку зосередитися на тому, як ми хочемо жити в майбутньому. Тому що незалежно від того, які можливості ми маємо в майбутньому, людина з усіма її потребами завжди повинна бути центром усіх змін, щоб життя було вартим того, аби жити в майбутньому».

A Meaningful Life After Recovering from Addiction – Future After No Future

Wolfgang Heckmann

In my field of expertise and experience – epidemiology, etiology, prevention and treatment of addictions – many of my colleagues stress the importance and influence of the term motivation:

- jeopardized (young) people are those who are less moti vated to seek qualification and work performance,
- addicted persons are those who lost all of their mo tivation and orientation to future except their day to day drug seeking behaviour,
- recovering from addiction is impossible without a per son's strong motivation for abstinence and soberness.

I am very much in doubt if motivation is the term of choice because I have seen so many different stades of motivation in one addicted person during only 24 hours of a day, that – in consequence – motivation is not a stable and reliable factor of the treatment process. The same person,

- who is highly motivated at noon, to see the doctor or the counsellor for beginning the treatment,
- comes along a drug using friend or a place where drugs are available, looses all the motivation immediately,
- is confronted later the day with his/her mother or spouse, who reinforces the will to undergo treatment,
- has to wait for the next morning, before the counselling centre opens again, fears or has withdrawal symptoms, uses more drugs,
- starts the day in bad mood but is still motivated for treatment,
- meets the counsellor at noon and makes plans for a future in abstinence,

- comes along a drug using friend or a place where drugs are available, looses all the motivation immediately,
- and so on and so on. Another turn.

In other words: Addiction is the strongest example for ambivalence or ambiguity conflicts (Lewin 1938) between appetence and aversion. It is not easy to predict, which side of the ambivalence has the lead at a certain moment.

Therefore I prefer in the context of motivational work and preparation for treatment the terms reason or target: Why should I stop my addictive behaviour? What is better or even as god as or at least nearly as god as the feeling of my favourite drug? What is worth all the efforts of undergoing treatment? What for is all that stress?

In my experience as a therapist I have seen all kinds of reasons to undergo or to continue treatment – very impressive and big ones as well as very small and trivial ones: I saw addicts quitting their behaviour because they wanted to finish their school or studies successfully, because they wanted to write a book or to become an actor, because they planned the marriage with the idol of their youth or because they wanted to live as a monk.

But also I saw quite often very small reasons like finding the way back to a former hobby like playing music with an instrument, like knowing, that a friend undergoes treatment in a certain facility and gets vocational training there, which might also be a chance. And even smaller reasons prevented a relapse during treatment, like the arrival of a new female client or the prospect to a visit of a swimming pool next day. To know why I start to change my life needs a target, which might be broken down to very small reasons to stay sober one more day.

Useful terms derived from research in social psychology and health promotion

The research of the social psychologist and co-founder of

humanistic psychology, Abraham H. Maslow, culminated in the early 40th of last century into a „Theory of Human Motivation" (Maslow 1943). As soon as it was published as a book, the „pyramid of needs" became very popular:

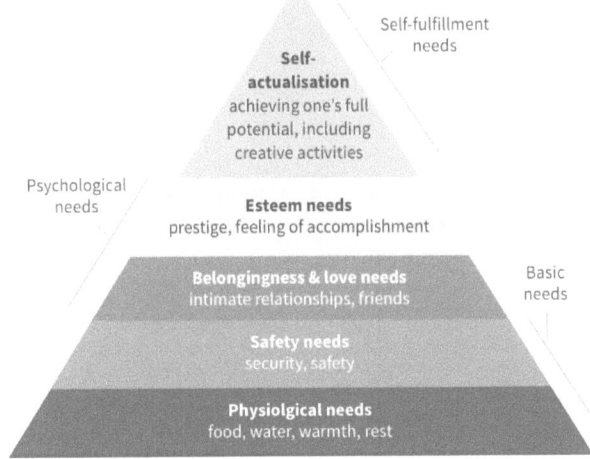

Figure 1: Maslow's Hierarchy of Needs (Maslow 1943, Source https://mrjoe.uk/assets/Maslows-Hierarchy-of-Needs.jpg)

The late Maslow himself added one more, the 6th step by using the term self-transcendence (cf. figure 2). On this step the person crosses the border of the self, of history, culture and environment and feels his/her connection to the undivided world. This leads to a very strong feeling of meaningfulness and opens the door to a peaceful development of myself and mankind (see Venter 2016).

There have been even more additions to the pyramid of needs, but to me the need for transcendence is the most important. It reminds me to a common experience of the early development of treatment in the field of drug dependency, mainly heroin addiction treatment.

Our understanding of addiction was a process of fleeing unbearable life conditions: Heroin as a very strong drug with

immediate effects of turning-down and switching-off all
perceptional and behavioural abilities was a very effective tool to
escape. Our answer was the Therapeutic Community as an offer of
social inclusion, which indeed answered a good deal of the needs
in the first four steps: physiological, safety, social and self-esteem
needs. And if self-actualisation started and was continuously
supported after treatment, sustainable social inclusion had a
chance (see Yablonsky 1967; Yablonsky 1989; Petzold/Vormann
1980; Heckmann 1980a, 1982a).

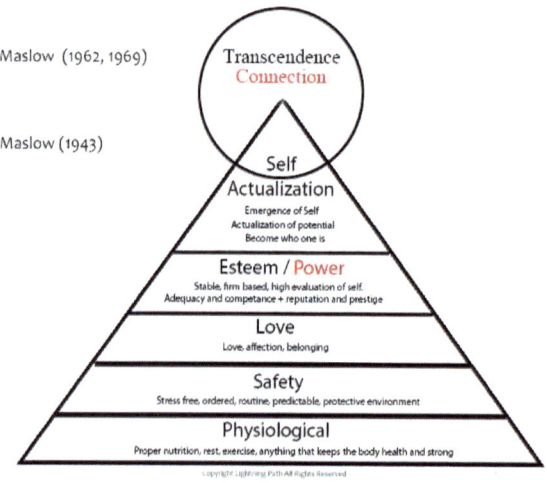

Figure 2: Extended Version (Source: Sosteric 2017)

It took years of successful development of treatment for addicts,
before we understood, that drug use is not only fleeing, but also
searching, a deep feeling of longing and yearning. Drug users are
not satisfied with circumstances, which most of the other people
at presence accept as given. And this lack of content is quite often
a lack of transcendence in a society, which loses religiosity, love,
charity and peace as values (see Heckmann 1980b, 1982a; Fleisch/
Haller/Heckmann 1997).

Health promotion was first and foremost an international movement: Healthy sports like jogging, cycling, swimming, care for healthy food and nutrition, deceleration of life and stress reduction came on the agenda. Self-help and action groups started their work in the industrialized countries during the 70s and 80s of the last century. The World Health Organisation published a handbook on self-help-groups and prepared their members for a summit in Ottawa 1986, which counts as the starting point for a change of perspectives on health worldwide.

Not only on a side note it should be mentioned, that already in the fourth and fifth decade of the last century self-help groups of alcoholics (Good Templars and Alcoholic Anonymous) have been spread out all over the globe.

One of the first and at least the most important researcher and theoretical contributor on the new health movement was Aaron Antonovsky. His term *sense of coherence* rose up to a key concept of health promotion very fast. Its elements: comprehensibility, manageability, and meaningfulness – this is a specialized terminology, which had to be memorized by generations of students since then. On the other hand it is quite easy to understand for those who are not well-educated: You feel more comfortable and familiar with a certain situation, the better you understand what is going on, the better you can trust that you will stand the situation, the better your feeling is that this all makes sense.

The relationship between this concept and our subject is self-explanatory, in particular because Antonovsky counts meaningfulness as one of three important factors for environmental health.

The environment of a drug user is the drug subculture. Within this scene he or she functions very well, but more like a machine as like a human being, as demographic research has illustrated very impressively (see Noller 1989).

All other situations of a regular day-to-day life are very stressful for addicts: low coherence, low comprehensiveness, low manageability, no meaningfulness. The above mentioned desire for a sense in life, even for transcendence is only maintained by drugs, not fulfilled. Treatment has to write the sense of coherence in bold letters.

Another term became recently more important than ever expected: *happiness* is no longer a trivial term but a term of significance for treatment purposes. The French psychiatrist Francois Lelord felt himself unhappy because he was not effective to treat all his patients so well, that they all became happy. He concluded, that he might not really know, what happiness could be. He decided to travel the world and to ask – as Hector – many people about their meaning of happiness. He collected in 23 chapters an impressive list of definitions for happiness – some are quite simple, others are very sophisticated: from „Happiness is wandering along beautiful unknown mountains" to „Happiness is sometimes not to understand everything" (Lelord 2002).

For myself, I used sometimes Hector's list – in seminars with students as well as in self-help groups of people with health problems or handicaps. It is astonishing, how motivating it can be, if a wide range of different offers for happiness is available and even small aspects of everybody's life might create happiness.

The last term to be presented here is *behaviour change*. Currently there is a variety of research findings and theoretical models available. They have all been tested in the field of health promotion and treatment, where behavioural change is the most appropriate or even crucial or indispensible choice – like in HIV / Aids prevention, prevention of lung cancer or, of course, misuse of drugs.

Among all the important contributions of researchers like Bandura, Becker, Ajzen, Fishbein, Rogers, Schwarzer or Weinstein (see BzgA 2016) for the field of drug prevention and treatment the *Transtheoretical Model* of Prochasca and di Clemente is the theory of choice.

This construct refers to the temporal dimension of behavioural change. In the transtheoretical model, change is a process involving progress through a series of stages:

- Precontemplation („not ready") – People are not intending to take action in the foreseeable future, and can be unaware that their behaviour is problematic
- Contemplation („getting ready") – People are beginning to recognize that their behaviour is problematic, and start to look at the pros and cons of their continued actions
- Preparation („ready") – People are intending to take action in the immediate future, and may begin taking small steps toward behaviour change
- Action – People have made specific overt modifications in modifying their problem behaviour or in acquiring new healthy behaviours
- Maintenance – People have been able to sustain action for at least six months and are working to prevent relapse
- Termination – Individuals have zero temptation and they are sure they will not return to their old unhealthy habit as a way of coping (Prochaska/di Clemente 2005).

It needs to be remarked that all stages are reversible: From a higher, more developed stage a person might go back to a lower stage or by chance comes back and goes a step forward. For counsellors and therapists it is of great importance, to understand where the client stands and not to overstrain him or her.

Between Prochaskas and di Clementes reasearch findings and one of the most popular tool in addiction counselling and treatment, the motivational interviewing (Miller/Rollnick 1991), there is a strong relationship. The early 90th of the last century have brought up in the field of drug treatment many efforts to overcome the confrontative style of treatment, as it was practiced in most of the Therapeutic Communities and many clinics. The democratic type of treatment facilities like in therapeutic communities of Ronald Laings or Maxwell Jones style have been quite rare.

In this situation the motivational interviewing as a non-confronting, client-centered method has been welcomed by a lot of experts. One of my PhD students, Günter Krauss, felt even earlier the need for a reform in drug treatment and worked out a method of not-patronizing counselling, which was very close to the MI-method (Krauss 1984). He was very experienced in counselling himself, but he also was ready to assist in developing a new era of treatment under the headline of humanity.

Pieces of current research on relations between meaningful life and addiction

One of my other PhD students, Stefan Thomas, conducted research among drug users, who lived on the streets of Berlin close to the railway station „Zoo". He tried to reconstruct the story of Christiane F., which has been first written down by two journalists in the late 70th of the last century (Hermann/Rieck 1979). He used ethnographic methods to get into a very close contact to a number of addicts on the streets around the station Zoo (Thomas 2008).

His main subject was the exclusion of young people, who decided to use drugs and to live on the streets. But the question was also about identity and meaningful life while living on the streets. Social identity is understood as that part of the individuals self-concept, which derives from their knowledge of their membership of a social group (or groups) together with the value and emotional significance attached to that membership. And in the Zoo stations scene there have only been three strategies of building identity been noticed:
- proof of ability to act by denial of reality
- giving up of ability to act by escaping reality
- partializing of ability to act by I-splitting

Identity under circumstances like these is split into an identity as drug user and successful dealer or machine-like junky on one hand and as a loser in terms of standing real life or of family contacts and friendship or mutual respect.

Identity has not been developed in the family or social environment of origin and cannot be developed in a social environment of failure and fear. Even on the streets the norms of the society like work performance and output are still of influence and the addicts are aware of their own exclusion.

Another PhD student did research on the relation of drug users and transcendental needs. He interviewed 10 drug users in depth and found a strong relationship to ideas of transcendence – not very explicit, but very authentic:

- Yes. I see myself only a part of a whole, which is not good or bad, maybe both.
- The good feeling under the influence of drugs is to leave leave this world which has only three dimensions.
- If I could cross the border without drugs I would do.
- I was very often close to death but also close to being immortal.
- Space and time are not stable, I loose myself in both oft hem and I find myself.
- I do not believe in God, but...
- Etc. (work still in progress).

Even if the research is not finished yet, it is foreseeable that most of the drug users seek in the illegal drugs something which they could not find by using alcohol and which is close to the term transcendence. And – as one of the interviewed persons expressed it – it might be necessary to find better ways of answers to transcendental needs to recover from addiction.

Experiences and confessions of former addicts

In various self-help-groups of addicts one term is of great importance: satisfactory abstinence. It sounds like a contradiction in itself, but it is of great importance to maintain a sober life. Therefore many of former addicts try – as a kind of self-assurance and reinforcement - speak in the meetings about their personal experiences with satisfactions. And again: The reasons are of great variety, small ones and big ones.

One of the most important techniques of self-affirmation seems to be the emphasis oft he positive aspects of abstinence like health, independant lifestyle, proudness (see Wossidlo 2017).

Whenever I meet former addicts they are full of stories about what makes them happy and satisfied:

- My former boss has hired me again.
- I was able to finish my studies.
- My family is back and I see the children growing.
- I saw the polar lights – as a drug user I would have never ever been able to travel that far.
- I am working in a clinic and support other addicts to accept treatment.

Some of these stories are really impressive. Our regional TV station recently interviewed a person who walked all the way from the North Pole through Greenland and the Americas down to Antarctica. It took years. And finally the man confessed that he before used to live for years on the streets as an alcoholic.

Last but not least: Every former addict likes to tell you exactly, how many days he or she is living sober: satisfaction by the number.

Personal remark

Another of my postgraduate students who is traveling a lot writes books about her experiences, for example on the pilgrim path of St. James, on her bicycle from northern to southern Finland etc. She also travelled through Albania asking a lot of people about their understanding of happiness.

She has her own podcast on the subject of traveling. Actually she is following up the aspects of traveling and escapism. For this purpose she did an interview with me about escapism and fleeing the boring everyday life. At the end she asked me about my personal view on happiness. My answer was: human closeness, consciousness, future.

References

Antonovsky, A. (1979): Health, stress and coping, San Francisco

Antonovsky, A. (1983): The sense of coherence: Development of a research instrument, Tel Aviv University

Antonovsky, A. (1987): Unrevealing the Mystery of Health. How people manage stress and stay well, San Francisco

Bundeszentrale für gesundheitliche Aufklärung (BzgA) (2016): Leitbegriffe der Gesundheitsförderung und Prävention, Köln

Falch, A.-B., Heckmann, W., Lisznyai, S. (2004): European Perspectives on Drug Addicted People, Frankfurt/Main

Fleisch, E., Haller, R., Heckmann, W. (1997): Suchtkrankenhilfe – Lehrbuch zur Vorbeugung, Beratung und Therapie, Weinheim und Basel

Heckmann, W. (1980a) Vielleicht kommt es auf uns selber an – Therapeutische Gemeinschaften für Drogenabhängige, Frankfurt/Main

Heckmann, W. (1980b): Eigentlich ist dieses Leben ein ständiger Hilferuf, in: Schaefers, C: Notausgänge, Hannover

Heckmann, W. (1982a): Jugendliche im Taumel vom Suchen zum Fliehen, in: Schlicht, U.: Trotz und Träume, Berlin

Heckmann, W. (1982b): Praxis der Drogentherapie – Von der Selbsthilfe zum Verbundsystem, Weinheim und Basel

Hermann, K. & Rieck, H. (2013): Zoo Station: The Story of Christiane F. (True Stories), San Francisco

Kraus, G.M. (1984): Konfliktberatung mit Drogenkonsumenten – Überlegungen zu einer Beratungsstrategie, Weinheim

Lelord, F. (2002): Hector and the Search for Happiness (Hector's Journeys), Rayleigh, UK

Lewin, K. (1938): The Conceptual Representation and the Measurement of Psychological Forces, Chicago, USA

Maslow, A.H. (1943): A Theory of Human Motivation. In Psychological Review York University, USA.

Maslow, A.H. (1953): Motivation and Personality, New York.

Miller, W. R. & Rollnick, S. (1991): Motivational interviewing: Preparing people to change addictive behavior, New York.

Naue, S. (2018): Suche zufriedene Abstinenz – suche Mut zu Neuem, A-Connect, Meinerzhagen.

Noller, P. (1989): Junkie-Maschinen – Rebellion und Knechtschaft im Alltag von Heroinabhängigen, Wiesbaden.

Petzold, H./Vormann, G. (1980): Therapeutische Wohngemeinschaften – Erfahrungen – Modelle – Supervision, München.

Prochaska, J. O. & di Clemente, C. C. (2005): The transtheoretical approach, in: Norcross, J. C. & Godfried, M. R.: Handbook of psychotherapy integration, New York, USA.

Sosteric, Marc: How to be human? Abraham Maslow and in hierarchies of need. In SoJourn 1/2017 (www.sociology.org/how-to-be-human/, Accessed on 15 February 2019).

Thomas, S. (2008): Exklusion und Selbstbehauptung - Eine (sozial-)psychologische Studie über Armut unter jungen Menschen auf der Straße, Freie Universität Berlin.

Venter, H.J. (2016). Self-Transcendence: Maslow's Answer to Cultural Closeness. Journal of Innovation Management, 4.

Yablonsky, Lewis (1967): The Tunnel Back, Los Angeles, USA.

Yablonsky, Lewis (1989): The Therapeutic Community – A Successful Approach for Treating Substance Abusers, Los Angeles, USA.

Wossidlo, C. (2017): Wie wird man zufrieden abstinent? Trokkenpresse, Heft 2.

Gesellschaftliche Teilhabe von Kindern mit Behinderungen und ihren Familien Gefahren - Chancen - Aufgaben

Hans- Dieter Dammering

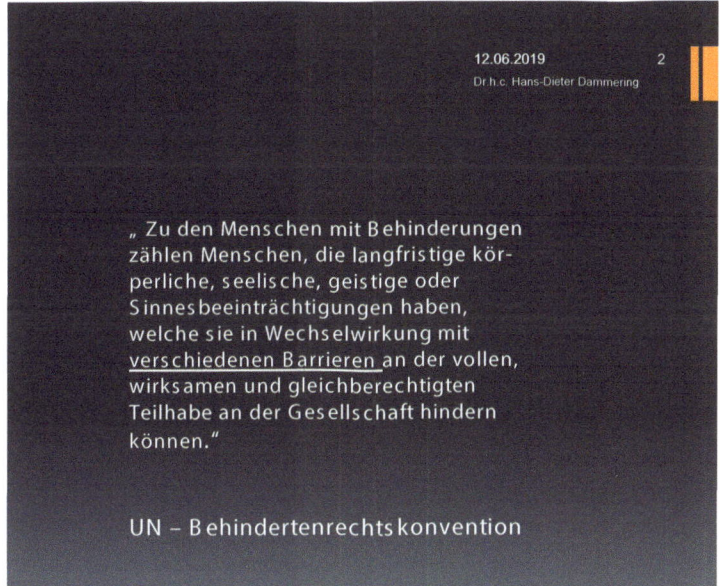

Kontextfaktoren zur Teilhabemöglichkeit

Gesamter Lebenshintergrund einer Person

- Umweltfaktoren
  Faktoren der materiellen, sozialen und
  verhaltensbezogenen Umwelt
- Personenbezogene (persönliche) Faktoren
  Eigenschaften und Attribute der Person
  (z.B. Alter, Geschlecht, Lebensstil,
  Motivation, genetische Prädisposition)

Funktionale Gesundheit und Kontextfaktoren

Kontextfaktoren (Umweltfaktoren, personbezogene Faktoren) können
sich auf die funktionale Gesundheit

- positiv auswirken (Förderfaktoren)

- negativ auswirken (Barrieren)

➤ Daher sind bei der Beurteilung der funktionalen Gesundheit einer
  Person stets ihre Kontextfaktoren zu berücksichtigen

Förderfaktoren zur Teilhabe

- Gemeinsam
  Bilden-Erziehen-Betreuen
- Anerkennung der Persönlichkeit
- kindzentrierte Pädagogik
- Differenzierte Angebote
- Akzeptanz des Andersseins

Barrieren zur Teilhabe

...in der Umwelt
...im Denken

- Ausgrenzung durch die Umwelt
- Rechte der Teilhabe werden nicht gedacht
- Förderangebote sind zu gering in Qualität und Quantität

Inklusion

Vollkommende Dazugehörigkeit

bildungs- , sozialpolitische und pädagogische Leitvorstellung;

anerkennt die grundsätzliche Einzigartigkeit und
Verschiedenheit aller Menschen sowie ihre
Zusammengehörigkeit in allen gesellschaftlichen
Lebensbereichen; ohne Ausgrenzung

Pädagogik der Vielfalt

… ein Weg zur kindzentrierten
Integrationspädagogik in der Institution

- Das individuelle Bedürfnis des Kindes entscheidet …

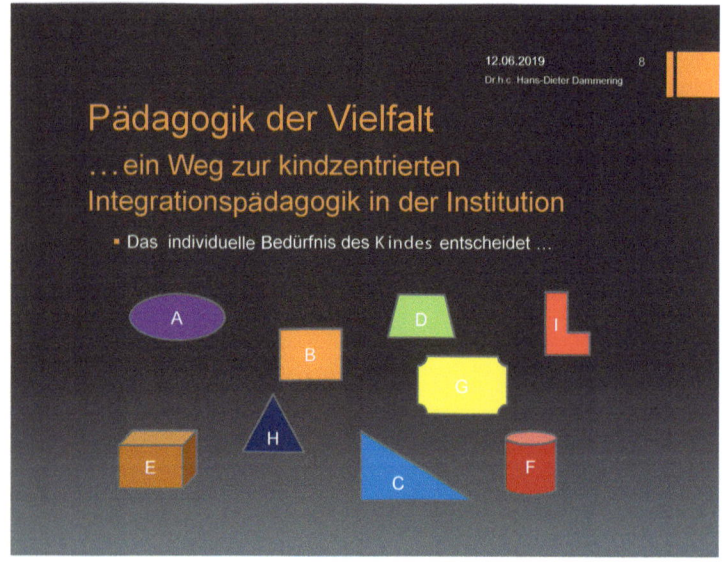

Pluralismus der Lebensformen
(Trend zu individualisierten Lebensstilen)
heute

- Ehepaar mit Kind
- Alleinstehend mit Kind
- Nichteheliche Lebensgemeinschaft
- Kinderlose Ehe mit Pflege- oder Adoptivkind
- getrenntes Zusammenleben
- Wohngemeinschaft
- Gleichgeschlechtliche Lebenspartnerschaft
- Wochenendehe
- Kinder mit mehreren (biologischen und sozialen) Müttern und Vätern
- Familien mit mehr als einer Partnerschaft

Besonderheiten
der Erziehungspartnerschaft
mit Eltern
von Kindern mit Behinderungen

12.06.2019   10
Dr.h.c. Hans-Dieter Dammering

- Es existiert ein erhöhter Beratungsbedarf
- Notwendigkeit der Begleitung in Konfliktsituationen
- Zukunftsangst von Eltern wahrnehmen
- Begleitung durch Individualisierung und Differenzierung bewusst realisieren

Thesen/ AUFGABEN

Integration / Inklusion verlangt:

- die Formulierung/ Anerkennung und Akzeptanz von Differenzierung und von besonderen Rechten von Kindern und Familien
- Die Einbindung in länderspezifischen Gesetzgebungsverfahren
- die Chance selbstbestimmt leben zu können
- die Reformierung pädagogischer Ausbildungsinhalte
- die Anerkennung und Verfügbarkeit des finanziellen Mehrbedarfes (personell / sächlich/ räumlich)
- die Durchsetzung des Selbstbestimmungsrechtes und einer Wahlmöglichkeit
- die Garantie zur Bereitstellung und Wahl einer Assistenz, die das Kind aufgrund seines Alters und der Behinderung benötigt

Suchen wir in unseren Kulturen
nach gemeinsamen,
humanistischen
Werten, welche für   den
E INZE LNE N
ein selbstbestimmtes
sinnvolles Leben ermöglichen !

Слайд 1

Участь дітей з інвалідністю та їх сімей в житті суспільства

Небезпеки – шанси – мети
2018

Слайд 2

„ До людей з інвалідністю належать особи зі стійкими фізичними, психічними, інтелектуальними або сенсорними порушеннями, які під час взаємодії з різними бар'єрами можуть заважати їх повній та ефективній участі в житті суспільства нарівні з іншими."

ООН – Конвенція про права осіб з інвалідністю

Контекстуальні фактори для можливості участі

Загальна життєва основа особи

- **Екологічні фактори**
  Фактори матеріального, соціального та поведінкового середовищ

- **Персоналізовані (особисті) фактори**
  Властивості та атрибути особи
  (наприклад, вік, стать, освіта, стиль життя, мотивація, генетична схильність

Функціональне здоров'я та контекстуальні фактори

Контекстуальні фактори (екологічні фактори, персоналізовані фактори) можуть здійснювати на функціональне здоров'я

- Позитивний вплив (фактори, що сприяють розвитку)

- Негативний вплив (бар'єри)

➢ А тому, при оцінюванні функціонального здоров'я особи треба завжди ураховувати її контекстуальні фактори.

Фактори, що сприяють zur Teilhabe

Клікнути для додання тексту

- <u>Спільно</u>
Освіта-виховання-патронаж
- Визнання особистості
- Педагогіка, у центрі якої дитина
- Диференційні пропозиції
- Акцептування інакшості

Бар'єри до участі

...в середовищі
...в мисленні

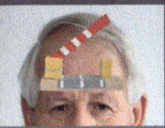

- Ізольованість з боку середовища
- Права на участь не враховуються
- Якість та кількість пропозицій для розвитку занадто незначні

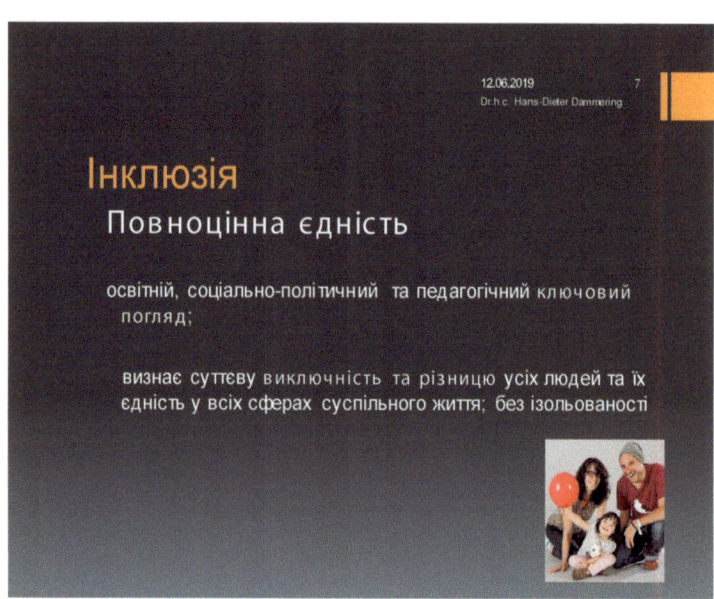

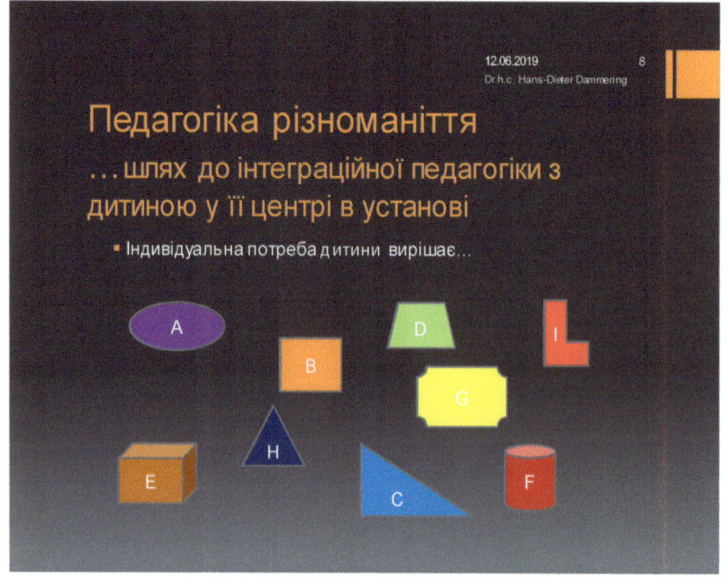

Плюралізм способів життя
(тенденція до індивідуалізованого способу життя) **сьогодні**

- Подружжя з дитиною
- Самотній з дитиною
- Спільне проживання однією сім'єю без шлюбу
- Шлюб без дітей з дитиною прийомною або на вихованні
- Окреме спільне проживання
- Житлова товариство
- Одностатеве партнерство
- Шлюб, в якому подружжя разом лише у вихідні дні
- Діти з декількома (біологічними та соціальними) матерями та батьками
- Сім'ї з більш ніж одним партнерством

Особливості партнерства у вихованні з батьками дітей з інвалідністю

12.06.2019   10
Dr.h.c. Hans-Dieter Dammering

- Існує підвищена потреба у консалтингу
- Необхідність супроводу у конфліктних ситуаціях
- Сприймати побоювання майбутнього у батьків
- Супровід свідомо реалізовувати через індивідуалізацію та диференціацію

Тезиси/ МЕТИ

Інтеграція/ інклюзія verlвимагаєangt:

- формулювання/ визнання та акцептування диференціації та особливих прав дітей та сімей
- <u>Включення</u> у спеціальне національне законодавство
- Шанс жити із самовизначенням
- Реформа змісту педагогічної освіти
- Визнання та наявність підвищеної фінансової потреби (кадрової/ матеріальної/ територіальної)
- Реалізація права на самовизнання та можливости вибору
- Гарантія надання та вибір допомоги, яку потребує дитина відповідно до свого віку та інвалідності

Давайте шукати в наших культурах спільні гуманістицні цінності, які дають кожній ОКРЕМІЙ ОСОБІ можливість жити усвідомлено та ein самовизначаючи!

Meaningful Life in the United States Social Rifts, Political Trends and Community Action

Frances Anne McPherson

Meaningful social connections, altruism and living life with purpose are essential elements of living a meaningful life.

Caring about the welfare of other people and acting to help them; enhancing the welfare of others without expectation of reward; serving/helping some cause greater than ourselves; contributing selflessly to make life a little better for those less fortunate.

Meaningful life in a democracy seeks to protect the weak and to empower people everywhere, so they can live their diverse lives freed from the tyranny of monarchs, oligarchs, authoritarianism and totalitarianism.

The United States was founded on liberal ideas – a democracy granting all voters the right to participate freely and fully in the life of their society.

Flawed democracy is not okay.
We have to call it out and talk about it.

Alarmingly, democracy in America appears in peril. Based on analysis of nearly 200 countries, the U.S. was downgraded from a "full democracy" to a "flawed democracy" in the Economist Intelligence Unit's 2016 Democracy Index and now again in the unit's 2017 Democracy Index.

"Mr. Trump has attacked the judiciary, ridiculed the media, defended torture, condoned police brutality … and equated mere policy disagreements with treason." Madeleine Albright Will We Stop Trump Before It's Too Late?

Former Secretary of State Madeleine Albright blasts the erosion of democracy under the presidency of Donald Trump, whom she

calls "the first anti-democratic president in modern U.S. history …
His words are so often at odds with the truth that they can appear
ignorant, yet are in fact calculated to exacerbate religious, social
and racial divisions."

Social Rifts

**The election of Donald Trump has proved a tragedy for
America's liberal democracy and a sickening event in the
history of the United States.**

In January 2018, the Washington Post reported that since Trump
was inaugurated, there has been a protest every day, somewhere in
the United States, spanning social issues. Under Donald Trump's
presidency, the polarizing divides between Republicans and Democrats on fundamental political values have reached record levels
and are growing even larger and more contentious. The magni-
tude of these differences dwarfs progressive efforts that seek to
move America forward toward a creative and innovative future—a
future that is cooperative globally and respectful of human rights.

**Anger, fear and confusion have resulted in deep social rifts,
characterized by rancor, mistrust and malevolence towards
those with whom we disagree.**

The nation is deeply divided over foreign policy. Democrats, and
others who value global cooperation, regard Trump's America
First slogan as toxic and are alarmed by his erratic conduct on the
world stage – his tweets and taunts, his cavalier disregard of international accords, his readiness to undercut his own diplomats,
his odd choice of friends, his disregard for diplomacy and his
increasingly militarized foreign policy. Republicans argue the U.S.
should pursue its own interests

**Trump's Department of Homeland Security has detained
and deported hundreds of thousands of immigrants.**

In defiance, major cities have declared sanctuary policies that mitigate enforcement.

Trump's war on immigrants divides the nation. Republican Anti-immigrant policies instill a fear that the country has been invaded by foreign criminals who are taking away their jobs and other resources. White supremacy speech and hate crimes increase in frequency. The President libels immigrants and the countries from which they come.

Most Americans say immigrants strengthen the country with their hard work and talents and most endorse granting permanent legal status to immigrants brought here illegally as children.

Health care in the United States lags behind the rest of the developed world in providing quality, affordable health care. High infant and maternal mortality rates contribute to a decrease in U.S. life expectancy.

Most Americans say access to health care is a basic human right. Soaring health costs and poorer outcomes cause crippling financial distress. Democrats push for universal healthcare. Congressional Republicans oppose government support for health care and have repeatedly tried to repeal ObamaCare. Pressure from their right-wing Evangelical base has led to Planned Parenthood funding cuts and laws limiting access to abortions.

Disastrous environmental agenda:
- maximizing the use of fossil fuels;
- dismantling regulations;
- sharply cutting back on research and development
- of alternative energy sources.
- Most Americans say dealing with climate change and protecting the environment should be a top policy priority. Environmentalists say Mr. Trump's climate change denial is catastrophic. There is great alarm that Republicans are un-

dermining environmental protections instead of increasing them. Democrats argue that stricter environmental laws and regulations are essential to cleaning up the environment and preserving forests and biodiversity. Hurricane-devastated Puerto Rico is in an ongoing environmental crisis with no federal help in sight.

No other society in human history has imprisoned so many of its own citizens.

Image.: Modern_Slavery.png (Source: http://news.infoshop.org/prisons/modern-day-slavery-in-the-usa/)

Most Democrats agree America must continue to make changes to give blacks equal rights with whites.
Republicans say blacks who can't get ahead are responsible for their own condition.

Racial discrimination in the United States is deplorable and has gotten worse since Mr. Trump's election. Racism has rooted in American culture – carried generation after generation. Systemic oppression is very real and very scary. According to findings of a Guardian study, young black men were nine times more likely than all other Americans to be killed by police. Human rights groups condemn as a form of slavery America's prison population of 2 million inmates – mostly Black and Hispanic – who are forced to work for pennies per hour. Inequality undermines basic human rights and leaves citizens feeling unsafe, alienated, and powerless within their own nation.

Gun violence in America

GUN MURDERS PER 100,000 RESIDENTS

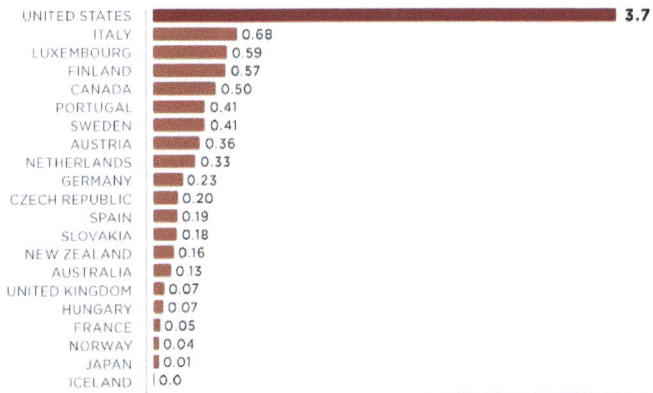

UNITED STATES	3.7
ITALY	0.68
LUXEMBOURG	0.59
FINLAND	0.57
CANADA	0.50
PORTUGAL	0.41
SWEDEN	0.41
AUSTRIA	0.36
NETHERLANDS	0.33
GERMANY	0.23
CZECH REPUBLIC	0.20
SPAIN	0.19
SLOVAKIA	0.18
NEW ZEALAND	0.16
AUSTRALIA	0.13
UNITED KINGDOM	0.07
HUNGARY	0.07
FRANCE	0.05
NORWAY	0.04
JAPAN	0.01
ICELAND	0.0

Image: GunViolence in USA (Source: https://everytownresearch.org/ wp-content/uploads/2015/08/USGunViolenceTrends_Chart1.png)

A majority of U.S. teens age 13 to 17 fear a shooting could happen at their school.
Gun control is favored by over 70% of the American public.

The FBI defines "mass shootings" as the injury or murder of four or more victims. CBS reported "nearly one mass shooting a day in 2017."

There were 18 school shootings during the first 6 weeks of this year – an average of 3 per week. The Parkland, Florida massacre that killed 17 people reignited a national debate about guns in America with public outcry demanding tighter gun laws. Republicans in Congress and the President continue to block gun reforms – their solution to school shootings is to arm teachers and post police at schools. The National Rife Association [NRA] contributes heavily to Republican candidates and lobbies lawmakers to prevent federal funding for gun violence research.

7000 pairs of children's shoes in front of the Capitol building representing all the children killed by gunfire since the Sandy Hook mass shooting in 2012.

Image: "Not one more" (Source: https://news.abs-cbn.com/overseas/multimedia/photo/03/14/18/not-one-more)

Political Trends

America's power structure appears less a liberal democracy and more an oligarchy.

Over recent decades, the nation's two main political parties have degenerated into sharply divided camps each recklessly undermining the other to the deterioration of democratic principles. To those of us who value democracy there is great alarm at the rise of nationalism in the United States – particularly among Republicans who are in control of all three branches of government.

America's Party of White Nationalism
Political nationalism: flag-waving xenophobes urging "patriots" to reclaim their homeland through border walls and armed local militia. Donald Trump: Burn the flag, go to jail.
Economic nationalism: "America First" policies control and manipulate prices to give clear advantages to U.S. companies.
The free press: assaulted as fake news and enemies of the truth.
Rule of law: trivializing white supremacy crime, interfering with the judiciary, condoning unlawful torture, trying to imprison political rivals and pardoning convicted criminals for personal political benefit.
Deregulation: rolling back hundreds of regulations designed to protect the environment, civil liberties and human rights.
Privatization: selling off the nation's assets to corporate entities who are motivated by profit over people.
Militarization: lusting for global military dominance.
Us/Them attitude: saying to the world: "Our way of life is more important than yours. Furthermore, we are willing to sacrifice your culture in order to promote our own."

What is to be done?
Defend the truth:
A free press is not the enemy of the American people; it is the protector of the American people.
Reinforce the rule of law:
No one, not even the president, is above the law.

Energize the democratic process:
Register new voters, listen respectfully to those with whom we disagree and work for projects that respect human rights and promote inclusion of marginalized populations.

Trends of Hope

Bernie Sanders is the most popular politician in the U.S.:
An outsider with no funding, condemned by the corporate media,

and an avowed socialist, fights for a progressive economic agenda that creates jobs, raises wages, protects the environment and provides health care for all.

Millennials are the largest voter-eligible age group:
The majority of Millennials overwhelmingly disapprove of President Trump, register as Independents and say they are energized to vote in the 2018 elections. Major focus is toward civil rights and helping to improve the lives of others.

Record number of Republican House members are not seeking re-election in 2018:
The 38 Republicans who are opting not to run for re-election this year are the most departures for the Republican Party since 1930. These departures, coupled with Mr. Trump's staggering unpopularity, have prompted speculation on Democrats' hopes of regaining control of this chamber.

Record number of women are running for office in state and local positions in 2018:
Women are fighting to have a voice at decision-making tables across America. Over 300 women have filed papers to run for seats in the U.S. House of Representatives this year. Likewise, a record number of female candidates are running in races for governor.

Community Action

What are Americans doing to meet the challenges of social rifts and the erosion of democracy?
Grassroots movements and projects that take responsibility for intercultural dialogue and stand up for inclusion of marginalized individuals and groups:

- Respect for Human Rights
- Women's March
- Pussyhat Project™

- Me Too Movement [#MeToo]
- Black Lives Matter
- Kaepernick's protest
- March for Our Lives
- National School Walkout
- Healthcare Is a Human Right
- Earth Day

A **Women's March** took place in Washington D.C. on the day following Trump's inauguration. In addition to D.C., women worldwide led massive marches to advocate legislation and policies regarding human rights and other issues. Most of the rallies were aimed at Donald Trump, largely in protest to statements he had made and his offensive, anti-women positions. As many as 4.6 million people took part in what is heralded as "the largest single-day protest in U.S. history". [Wikipedia]

The **Pussyhat Project™**: A group of women in Los Angeles began knitting hats to be worn at the Women's March as a symbol of support and solidarity for women's rights. This local political resistance project quickly spread online and united millions at Women's Marches around the world. It has grown into a social movement focused on raising awareness about women's issues and advancing human rights.

Me Too is a protest movement against sexual harassment and rape, begun by a social activist and community organizer as part of a grassroots campaign to reach out to sexual assault survivors in underprivileged communities. Hashtag #MeToo spread virally on social media in October last year as part of an awareness campaign to reveal the widespread prevalence of sexual assault and harassment, especially in the workplace.

Black Lives Matter is an international activist movement, originating in the African-American community, that campaigns against violence and systemic racism towards black people. BLM regularly holds protests speaking out against police killings of black people, and broader issues such as racial profiling, police brutality, and racial inequality in the United States criminal justice system.

This year, Amnesty International gave former NFL quarterback Colin Kaepernick its Ambassador of Conscience Award for his **kneeling protest of racial injustice** that launched a sports movement. Other players joined his protest during the 2016 football season, infuriating President Trump, who called for team owners to fire players who kneel during the National Anthem. In response to player demonstrations, the NFL has committed $90 million to social justice causes.

March for Our Lives: Just five weeks after a gunman killed 17 of their friends and teachers at a Florida high school, students organized, then led, this historic march which has launched a mass movement toward national gun control. March for Our Lives organizers estimate 800,000 protesters attended the gun-control demonstration in Washington, D.C. in March this year, with over 800 sibling events throughout the United States and around the world. Parkland students have become social activists. Their Go-FundMe Campaign raised 3.7 million dollars in just three days. They've designated these donations to fight for comprehensive gun safety laws to protect demanding America's kids from gun violence.

National School Walkout is a student created and student led, the movement calls on fellow young people to push for gun control legislation. Students from more than 2,500 schools across the country walked out of classrooms to demand action on gun reform. The event took place on the 19th anniversary of the Columbine High School massacre in Colorado when a gunman killed 12 students and a teacher.

Healthcare Is a Human Right is a people's movement organizing state by state to win universal, publicly financed healthcare as a public good that belongs to us all. This collaborative movement, founded on a principle of people's needs ahead of profits, was formed by grassroots groups in Vermont, Maine, Maryland, and

Pennsylvania and now exists in several U.S. states. In 2011, Vermont became the first state to pass a law for a universal, publicly financed health care system.

- Living a meaningful life matters.
- Defending civil liberties and human rights matters.
- The choices we make and the roles we play in this tapestry of life matter.
- Every single life matters.
- Every single life makes a difference.
- What sort of difference our lives make is a personal choice.

Daniel W. Bloemers

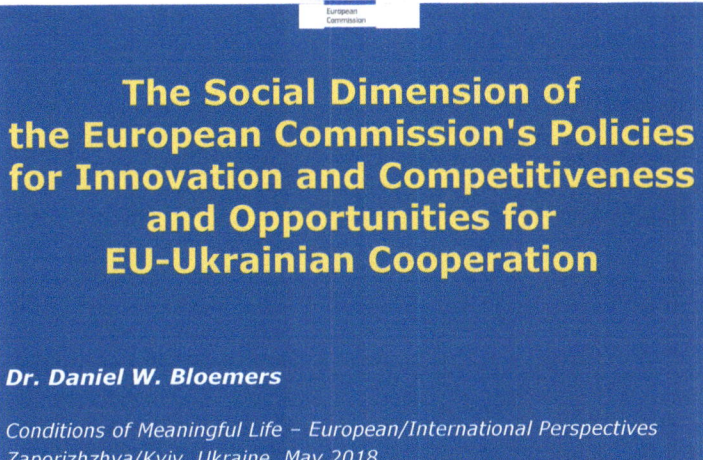

The Social Dimension of the European Commission's Policies for Innovation and Competitiveness and Opportunities for EU-Ukrainian Cooperation

Dr. Daniel W. Bloemers

Conditions of Meaningful Life – European/International Perspectives
Zaporizhzhya/Kyiv, Ukraine, May 2018

Conditions of meaningful life

- *What are (the) conditions of meaningful life?*
- *Who has to create them?*
- *What does the European Union contribute to creating them?*
- *What does the EU do in/for Ukraine?*

The EU is working for a more united, stronger and more democratic Europe.

Context

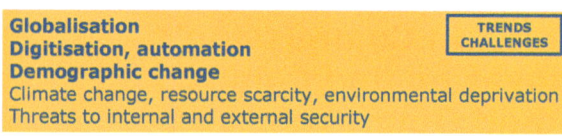

Globalisation
Digitisation, automation
Demographic change
Climate change, resource scarcity, environmental deprivation
Threats to internal and external security

TRENDS CHALLENGES

Increasing global competition
Societal transformation
Changing nature of work
Changing roles of individuals

IMPLICATIONS

Productivity, value creation, global competitiveness
Sustainable production and consumption
Security
Social cohesion
Meaningful life for all individuals

PRIORITIES OBJECTIVES

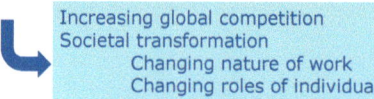

Priorities of the European Commission

Jobs and growth: stimulate investment, remove obstacles
Internal Market: deepen the core of EU integration
Digital Single Market: unlock online opportunities
Monetary Union: stability, fairness and accountability
Trade: harness globalisation, safeguard European standards
Energy: more secure, affordable and sustainable
Justice and fundamental rights: cooperation and rule of law
Migration: towards a European agenda
Democratic change: better regulation, visions for the future
External action: common foreign policy

https://ec.europa.eu/commission/priorities_en

"It is up to us to ensure that the handwriting of the European Social Model is clearly visible in everything we do. Because Europe is the protective shield for all of us who can call this magnificent continent their home."

European Commission President Jean-Claude Juncker, Speech before the European Parliament, 22 October 2014

Social dimension in all policies
Social legislation
Fair and enforceable labour mobility
Youth and skills

https://ec.europa.eu/commission/sites/beta-political/files/social_priorities_juncker_commission_en.pdf

---

EU Pillar of Social Rights

Building a more inclusive and fairer European Union

- **Equal opportunities and access to the labour market**
  Education, training and life-long learning; Gender equality; Equal opportunities; Active support to employment

- **Fair working conditions**
  Secure and adaptable employment; Wages; Information about employment conditions and protection in case of dismissals; Social dialogue and involvement of workers; Work-life balance; Healthy, safe and well-adapted work environment and data protection

- **Social protection and inclusion**
  Childcare and support to children; Social protection; Unemployment benefits; Minimum income; Old age income and pensions; Health care; Inclusion of people with disabilities; Long-term care; Housing and assistance for the homeless; Access to essential services

https://ec.europa.eu/commission/priorities/deeper-and-fairer-economic-and-monetary-union/european-pillar-social-rights_en

Social innovation

Social innovations

- New ideas that meet social needs, create social relationships and form new collaborations
- Products, services or models addressing unmet needs

European Social Innovation Competition

https://ec.europa.eu/growth/industry/innovation/
policy/social_en

Social Innovation Competition

Winners 2017:

- Collaborative platform offering individuals and local communities knowledge and tools to design and build sustainable homes
- Multimedia tool allowing blind and visually-impaired people to feel shapes on a flat screen
- Peer-to-peer learning network for users to learn in-demand tech skills from industry experts

https://ec.europa.eu/growth/industry/innovatio
policy/social/competition_en

Future of Europe: the social dimension

How to...
... sustain our standard of living?
... create more and better jobs?
... equip people with the right skills?
... create more unity within our society?

Three scenarios:
- *Limit the social dimension to free movement*
- *Those who want to do more in the social field do more*
- *The EU27 deepen the social dimension of Europe together*

https://ec.europa.eu/commission/publications/
reflection-paper-social-dimension-europe_en

EU-Ukraine relations (I)

- Ukraine: **priority partner** for the European Union; bilaterally and within the EU's Eastern Partnership
- Unwavering support for **territorial integrity and sovereignty**
- **Association Agreement** (since 1 September 2017):
    - Political ties, economic links, respect for common values
    - Implementation monitored annually
    - Deep and Comprehensive Free Trade Area:
      Ukrainian businesses receive preferential access to the world's largest market (Imports and exports EU⮂ UA, +27% in 2017)
    - Trigger for reform of Ukraine's legal framework
      → alignment with EU *acquis*

https://eeas.europa.eu/delegations/
ukraine/1937/ukraine-and-eu_en

EU-Ukraine relations (II)

- Ambitious **reform** timetable:
  stabilise economy and improve the livelihoods of citizens
- Top priorities:
  - Fight against corruption
  - Judiciary reform
  - Constitutional and electoral reforms
  - Improvement of the business climate
  - Improvement of energy efficiency
  - Reform of public administration, including decentralisation
  - Gender mainstreaming
- EUR 12.8 billion of EU support for reform process
- **Visa-free travel** for Ukrainian citizens: facilitate people-to-people contacts; strengthen business, social and cultural ties

EU-UA: social policies

- Implementation of Association Agreement
- Approximation of Ukrainian legislation to EU directives and best practices
  - New models of service delivery to vulnerable groups
  - Projects implemented by civil society organisations
  - Capacity development for social service providers: NGOs and social workers
- Twinning led by *Expertise France*: system of early intervention and rehabilitation for children with disabilities

EU-UA: research and innovation

- Integration of Ukraine into **European Research Area**
- EU supports reform and modernisation of Ukrainian national research and innovation system
- Association to EU Framework Programme **"Horizon 2020"**: Ukrainian researchers, businesses and innovators can apply on equal terms with their EU counterparts

Ukraine is not yet benefitting to the maximum ☐ need to:
- **Build networks with EU partners**
- **Orient towards EU priority topics**
- **Implement policy recommendations**

http://ec.europa.eu/research/era/index_en.htm
http://ec.europa.eu/programmes/horizon2020/

Peer Review of the Ukrainian Research and Innovation System

Recommendations:
1. Increase research investment
2. Cross-governmental science strategy
   → key to future growth and societal well-being
3. Science and research for the benefit society
   → to be anchored in the mission and rules of research bodies
4. Clear and quick decisions on priorities
5. Institutional revamp of science bodies, funding and procedures
6. Open up to international projects, leverage Horizon 2020
7. Open communication about reform process

https://rio.jrc.ec.europa.eu/en/policy-support-facility/peer-review-ukrainian-research-and-innovation-system

141

EU-UA: education / "people-to-people"

- Integration of Ukraine into **European Higher Education Area**
- EU supports reforms to modernise the education system:
  → deliver globally-recognised, quality education
  → expand internationalisation
- **Erasmus+**: active participation in EU capacity-building and academic mobility schemes
  - International and intercultural experiences of students and staff
  - Familiarisation with new learning and teaching methods
  - Strengthening of competences and networks

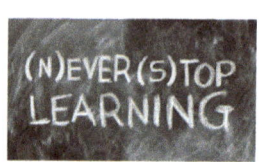

http://www.ehea.info/
http://ec.europa.eu/programmes/erasmus-plus/node_en

EU projects in Ukraine

- 250 projects across sectors, regions and cities
- EU: biggest donor in Ukraine; EUR 12 billion in last three years
- 77% of Ukrainians are unaware of EU programmes

https://eeas.europa.eu/delegations/ukraine/area/projects_en

Vice-President/High Representative Federica Mogherini at Taras Shevchenko National University of Kyiv

"The European Union has been, is and will continue to be here every day by your side, consistently bringing big, small, big results in everyday life. We have committed to our friendship with Ukraine again and again."

"Important steps have been taken in these years and some important reforms have been passed. But more reforms will be necessary [...] this is not something that Brussels asks; this is something that Ukrainians ask."

Dr. Daniel W. Bloemers

Policy Officer / International Relations Officer
Daniel-Wolf.BLOEMERS@ec.europa.eu
Tel.: (+32 2 29) 64992

Digitale Medien im Vordergrund: Deutsche und ukrainische Studierende im Vergleich

Nina Rodefeld, Pascale Schinkitz & Aaron Schäfer

Mit einem Bildungsauftrag unter dem Themenschwerpunkt „Medien und Demokratie in der Ukraine", ging es für 11 Studierende der Sozialen Arbeit von der Hochschule Magdeburg-Stendal im Juni 2018 zu einer Exkursion nach Perejaslaw-Chmelnyzkyi (Переяслав-Хмельницький). Die Hochschule Magdeburg-Stendal und die Pädagogische Universität „Gregorij Skovoroda" sind Partneruniversitäten und pflegen einen regelmäßigen Austausch von Studierenden und Wissenschaftler*innen, der vom Deutschen Akademischen Austauschdienst – DAAD im Rahmen des Programmes Ost-West-Dialogs seit 2014 gefördert wird.

Innerhalb des Projektes bildeten sich mehrere Kleingruppen, die sich mit verschiedenen Themen im Bereich der Medien und Demokratie beschäftigten. Drei Studierende entschlossen sich, eine Befragung bezüglich des Medienverhaltens bei Studierenden in der Universität in Perejaslaw durchzuführen. Die gleiche Befragung führten dann im November desselben Jahres ukrainische Studierende an der Hochschule Magdeburg-Stendal in Magdeburg durch.

Die Befragung bezog sich auf das individuelle Medienverhalten in der Freizeit und die Mediennutzung in der Universität. Des Weiteren ging es um verschiedene Apps, die die Befragten auf ihren Smartphones besitzen und wofür sie überwiegend genutzt werden.

Das Ziel der Befragung war es, eventuelle Unterschiede wie auch Gemeinsamkeiten in den verschiedenen Ländern festzustellen.

Teilnehmer/Innen

An der Befragung in der Universität in Perejslaw nahmen 35 Studentinnen und 4 Studenten im Alter zwischen 17 und 22 Jahren teil. Die meisten von ihnen studierten zu dem Zeitpunkt Deutsche Sprache und Literatur, aber auch andere Sprachen wie Französisch oder Englisch.

In Deutschland, an der Hochschule Magdeburg Stendal, nahmen 34 Studentinnen und 17 Studenten teil. Das Alter erstreckte sich hierbei von 18 bis hin zu 28 Jahren. Dabei handelte es sich um Studierende des Fachbereichs Soziale Arbeit, Gesundheit und Medien.

Interessante Antworten und Ergebnisse

Die erste Frage bezog sich auf die verschiedenen Medien, welche genutzt werden (siehe Diagramm 1). Die Auswertung in der Ukraine ergab, dass alle Teilnehmer (39 von 39) das Smartphone am häufigsten nutzen. Knapp danach folgen für 38 der 39 Befragten die Benutzung des Laptops und des PCs. Für immerhin 29 von 39 befragten Studierenden spielt das Medium der Bücher eine größere Rolle. In Deutschland kam es zu ähnlichen Ergebnissen wie in der Ukraine: 50 von 51 Studierenden nutzen ein Smartphone, 49 von ihnen nehmen einen Laptop oder PC zur Hilfe und 40 Studierende geben an, dass sie Bücher tagtäglich verwenden.

Eine Überraschung während der Auswertung brachte uns die Frage, wie lange die Befragten ihre Zeit am Tag im Internet verbringen (siehe Diagramm 2). Zur Auswahl standen die Möglichkeiten: „0-1 Stunde am Tag“, „2-4 Stunden am Tag“, „4-6 Stunden am Tag“, „6-8 Stunden am Tag“ sowie über „8 Stunden am Tag“. Entgegen der Erwartungen waren die Antworten in beiden Fällen, also sowohl in der Ukraine als auch in Deutschland, gleich. Die Vertreter der beiden Universitäten gaben an, dass sie nur 4-6 Stunden im Internet am Tag Zeit verbringen. Wenn man bedenkt, welche Möglichkeiten die medialen Geräte heutzutage bieten und dass Studierende immer mit solchen in Kontakt treten, sei es bei der Recherche von wissenschaftlichen Artikeln oder bei der Ausarbeitung in der Bibliothek, sind 4-6 Stunden am Tag eine vergleichsweise kurze Zeit.

Eine weitere Frage bezog sich auf die App-Nutzung der Studierenden (siehe Diagramm 3). Bei den Studierenden in Deutschland war die App „WhatsApp", also ein Messenger-Dienst, mit dem man mit Freund*innen schreiben, Bilder/Videos versenden oder Sprachmemos und genaue Standorte verschicken kann, die meistgenutzte (51/51 Nennungen). Direkt im Anschluss lag „Instagram" mit 35 Nennungen auf dem zweiten Platz und gefolgt von „Youtube" mit 34 Nennungen. Bei der Befragung in der Ukraine zeigte sich hingegen „Youtube" als meist genutzte App der Studierenden (36/39 Nennungen), auf Platz zwei „Viber" (ein mit „WhatsApp" vergleichbarer Messenger-Dienst) mit 34 Nennungen. Wie auch bei den Magdeburger Studierenden ist in der Ukraine „Instagram" sehr beliebt (32/39 Nennungen).

Am Ende des Fragebogens ging es um die Frage, ob alle Studierenden die gleichen Möglichkeiten haben, digitale Medien zu nutzen (siehe Diagramm 4). Mögliche Antworten waren folgende: „Stimme voll zu", „Stimme eher zu", „Weiß nicht", „Stimme eher nicht zu" und „Stimme überhaupt nicht zu". In beiden Fällen kamen nahezu ähnliche Resultate zu Stande. Viele Studierende finden, dass nicht alle die gleichen Möglichkeiten haben, was die mediale Nutzung betrifft.

Fazit und Ausblick

Als Fazit der Befragung lässt sich sagen, dass entgegen vieler Annahmen die Mediennutzung der befragten Studierenden in der Ukraine und in Deutschland nahezu identisch ist. Anscheinend haben sie die gleichen Gewohnheiten: Die Apps, die sie nutzen, um in Verbindung zu bleiben und sich Informationen zu holen, sind sich im Ganzen sehr ähnlich. Etwas unterschiedlich ist die Bewertung des Zugangs zu digitalen

Medien für alle. Während Studierenden in Deutschland die Möglichkeit der uneingeschränkten Nutzung von PC-Poolen in der Universität haben, scheint das in der Ukraine anders zu sein. Warum dies so ist, ließ sich in unserer Befragung leider nicht herausfinden. Auch wäre es interessant zu wissen, aus welchen Medien die Studierenden Informationen bekommen, die sie als seriös betrachten.

Diagramm 1

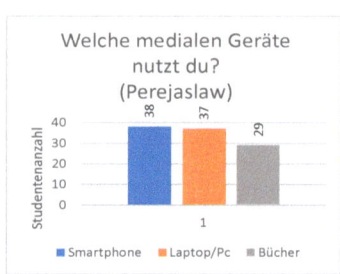
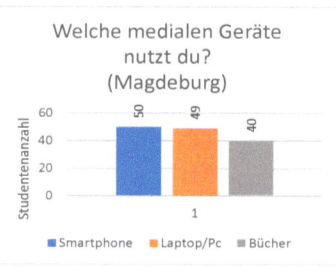

Diagramm 2

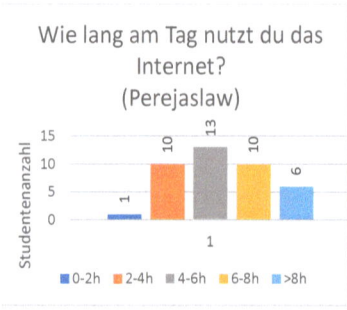
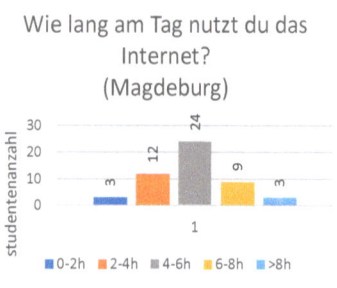

Diagramm 3

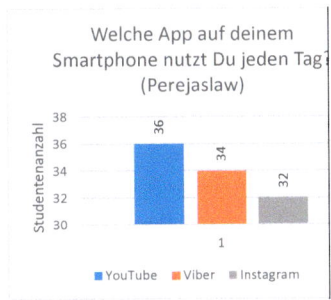

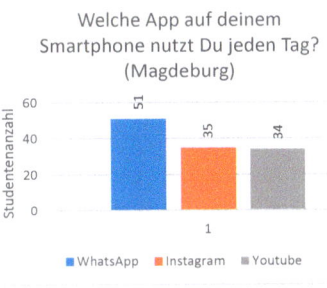

Diagramm 4

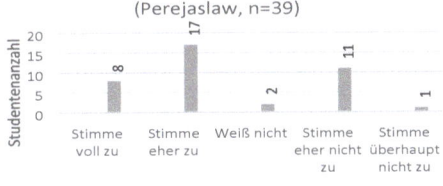

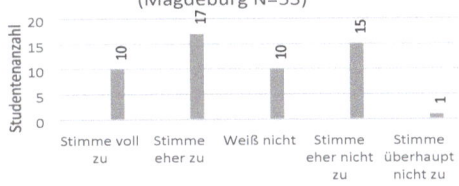

У фокусі цифрові засоби масової інформації: порівняємо, котрим з них надають перевагу німецькі, а котрим українські студенти

У червні 2018р. 11 студентів факультету Соціальна робота університету Магдебург-Стендаль вирушили у Переяслав-Хмельницький з освітнім завданням по темі «Засоби масової інформації та демократія в Україні». Починаючи з 2014р. університети-партнери Магдебург-Стендаль та Педагогічний університет ім. Григорія Сковороди проводять обмін студентами та науковцями завдяки фінансуванню, яке надає Німецька служба академічних обмінів (нім. Deutscher Akademischer Austauschdienst (DAAD)) в рамках програми Діалог Схід-Захід,

В ході реалізації проекту студенти поділились на маленькі групи, які працювали над різними темами зі сфери засобів масової інформації та демократії. Троє студентів вирішили провести опитування серед студентів переяславського університету щодо співвідношення різних засобів масової інформації, якими ті користуються. У листопаді того ж року українські студенти провели аналогічне опитування в університеті Магдебург-Стендаль у Магдебурзі.

Опитування стосувалось індивідуального використання засобів масової інформації на дозвіллі та під час навчального процесу в університеті. Йшлося також про різні мобільні додатки, наявні у смартфонах опитуваних, а також про те, для чого вони переважно використовуються. Метою опитування було визначити, що спільного та відмінного є в обох країнах.

Учасники

У переяславському університеті було опитано 35 студенток та 4 студенти у віці від 17 до 22 років. Більшість з них на той момент вивчала німецьку мову та літературу, а також інші мови, як, наприклад, французька та англійська.

У Німеччині в університеті Магдебург-Стендаль опитуванням були охоплені 34 студентки та 17 студентів у віці від 18 до 28 років. У цьому випадку йшлося про студентів факультету Соціальна робота, здоров'я та засоби масової інформації.

Цікаві відповіді та результати

Перше питання було про види засобів інформації, якими користуються опитувані (див. діаграму 1). Опитування в Україні показало, що всі учасники (39 з 39) найчастіше використовують смартфон. З невеликою різницею, а саме, 38 з 39 учасників опитування назвали ноутбук та комп'ютер на другому місці за використанням після смартфону. Однак для 29 з 39 опитаних студентів книжки як засіб інформації відіграють більшу роль. Опитування у Німеччині показало подібний результат: 50 з 51 студента користуються смартфоном, 49 з них звертаються за допомогою до ноутбука або ПК, а ще 40 студентів відзначили, що користуються кожного дня книжками.

При аналізі результатів опитування несподіванкою стала відповідь на питання про кількість часу, який опитувані проводять щоденно в Інтернеті(див. діаграму 2). Були запропоновані на вибір наступні відповіді: „0-1 година на день", „2-4 години на день", „4-6 годин на день", „6-8 годин на день" , а також понад „8 годин на день". Беручи до уваги ті можливості, які на сьогоднішній день надають медійні пристрої і те, що студенти постійно мають справу з такими пристроями, незалежно від того, шукають вони наукові статті чи самі займаються науковими розробками у бібліотеці, 4-6 годин в Інтернеті на день – це порівняно короткий час.

Інше питання стосувалось використання студентами мобільних додатків (див. діаграму 3). Студенти з Німеччини (51/51) назвали „WhatsApp", тобто месенджер, за допомогою якого можна листуватись з друзями, відправляти фото/відео або звукові повідомлення та повідомляти точні географічні координати, найбільш використовуваним мобільним додатком. На другому місці розташувався „Instagram" з 35 голосами, а слідом за ним „Youtube“ з 34 голосами. Опитування в Україні показало, що найчастіше студенти користуються саме додатком „Youtube“ (36/39 опитаних), на друге місце 34 голосами українські студенти поставили „Viber“ (месенджер подібний до „WhatsApp“). В Україні, як і серед студентів Магдебурга, дуже полюбляють „Instagram“ (32/39 згадувань).

Опитувальний лист завершувало питанням про те, чи всі студенти мають рівні можливості користуватись цифровими засобами інформації (див. діаграму 4). Відповідь слід було вибрати серед таких можливих: „повністю погоджуюсь“, „швидше погоджуюсь“, „не знаю“, „швидше не погоджуюсь“ та „взагалі не погоджуюсь“. Результати обох опитувань виявились подібними. Багато студентів вважають, що не всі мають однакові можливості використання медіа-засобів.

Підсумок і завдання

Підводячи підсумки опитування, слід сказати, що на відміну від численних припущень, опитані українські та німецькі студенти використовують засоби інформації майже ідентично.

Вони, очевидно, мають однакові звички: мобільні додатки, якими вони користуються, щоб залишатись на зв'язку та стягувати інформацію, в цілому дуже подібні. Дещо відрізняється оцінювання загального доступу до цифрових засобів інформації. Якщо німецькі студенти мають можливість необмеженого користування комп'ютерними класами, то в Україні це виглядає інакше. Чому це так, наше опитування вияснити, на жаль, не дозволяло. Було би також цікаво дізнатись, з яких засобів інформації студенти черпають інформацію, яку вважають серйозною.

Діаграма 1:

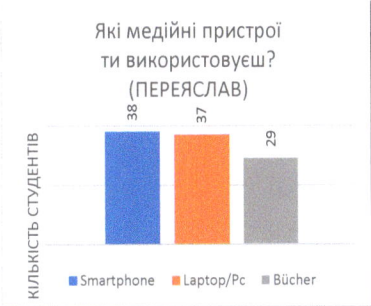

Діаграма 2:

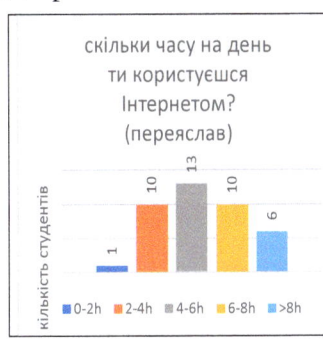

Діаграма 3:

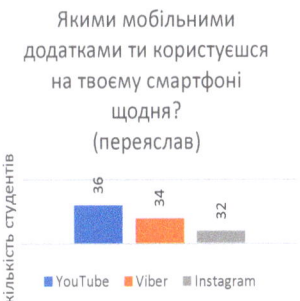

Діаграма 4:

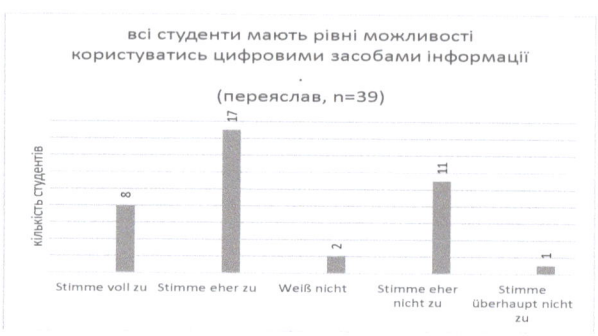

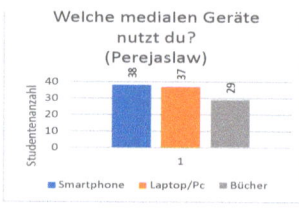 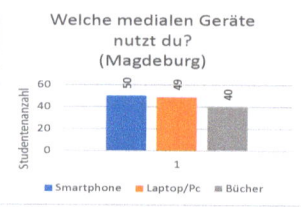

"Stimme voll zu"........................ „повністю погоджуюсь"
"Stimme eher zu"....................... „швидше погоджуюсь"
"Weiß nicht"............................... „не знаю"
"Stimme eher nicht zu"............ „швидше не погоджуюсь"
Stimme überhaupt nicht zu"... „взагалі не погоджуюсь"

Authors/Abstracts
(in alphabethical order)

Daniel W. Bloemers
Dr. of Business Economics (International Innovation Management); International Relations Officer, European Commission, Brussels, Belgium, and visiting lecturer at University of Wroclaw, Poland

The Social Dimension of the European Commission's Policies for Innovation and Competitiveness and Opportunities for EU-Ukrainian Cooperation

Starting from a reflection on conditions of meaningful life against the backdrop of globalisation, digitisation, automation, demographic change, and environmental challenges, he outlined the European Commission's policy priorities, zooming in on selected initiatives in the social dimension, before elaborating on EU-Ukraine relations. Mr Bloemers stressed that the European Union regards Ukraine as a priority partner, as exemplified by the ongoing implementation of an ambitious association agreement in force since September 2017. Quoting the European Union's High Representative for Foreign Affairs and Security Policy and Vice-President of the European Commission, Federica Mogherini, Mr Bloemers concluded that important steps in EU-Ukraine cooperation have been taken in recent years, but that more reforms will be necessary to unlock the potential of Ukraine and create conditions of meaningful life for all Europeans.

Wolf Bloemers
Prof. Dr. Dr. h.c. et Prof. h.c. mult., Dr. of Pedagogy, Analytical Psychotherapist, Professor em. of Special Pedagogy, University of Applied Scences Magdeburg-Stendal, Germany

Meaningful Life in Times of Worldwide Clashes, Tremors and Uncertainties. An Outline of Analysis and of Giving Directions

The text is the Keynote address given to the International Conference "Conditions of Meaningful Life – European/International Perspectives", held at Taras Shevchenko National University of Kiev in May 2018. Starting from shocking, oppressive photos showing current realities of poverty, starvation, unemployment, civil war, terrorism, migration, ecological devastation, the presentation traces questions about "what is a meaningful life?" and how to win this by sketching summarily our present "world in turmoil", by outlining some theories and some current empirical research results dealing with the questions of a meaningful life, and finally tries to derive from these answers some conditions, offers and signposts for personal giving meaning and by means of selected thought splinters from psychologists.

Olena Chuiko
Doctor of Psychological Sciences (PhD), Professor and head of the department of Social Rehabilitation and Social Pedagogy, Taras Shevchenko National University of Kyiv, Ukraine

Особистісне становлення студентів соціономічних професій - Personal formation of the students of socionomical professions

In the article, researchers are trying to find the correlation between education and personal maturity. Questions that were asked in the study include, inter alia, „Is the formation of personal maturity possible at the university?", „Is it possible to "accelerate" maturity of the personality?" and „What education should be that will "start" the process of personal maturity (technology of "shift of age frame")?".
With the concept of personal formation of the subject of professional activity as well as projects designed and conducted by questioned students, results of the study were the following: The most pronounced changes in the value-notional sphere is that the past (studying at the university) is evaluated as value, where productive self-realization and realization of opportunities take place. There is also a tendency for self-acceptance as well as developing positive dynamics in a personal communicative sphere.

Irina Crumpei
Doctor of Psychology (PhD), Assist.-Professor
and **Ion Dafinoiu**
Dr. of Psychology , Psychotherapist, Professor, both at Faculty of Psychology, Alexandru Ioan Cuza University, Iaşi, Romania

Social Representations of the Elderly in Romania

The recent decades face an important demographic transition as the population is constantly ageing and the birth rate decreases. The subject of aging presents a growing interest in the scientific community. Our study aimed to clarify Romanian social representations of the elderly. 76 participants were submitted to an inductive method using the ambiguous scenario and an associative map task. Results show that associations split between physical and psychological changes. Illness and helplessness are elements associated with physical decline, while wisdom, loneliness and grandparenthood are related to psychosocial perception. Elderly women are perceived as more vulnerable, being significantly more likely to suffer from loneliness, lack of money or health problems compared to elderly men or even adult men and women.

Hans-Dieter Dammering

Dr. h.c. of Pedagogy, Director of the integrated day care facility "Kuschelhaus", Magdeburg, Germany.

Gesellschaftliche Teilhabe von Kindern mit Behinderungen und ihrer Familien
Участь дітей з інвалідністю та їх сімей в житті суспільства

Due to UN's Convention on the Rights of Persons with Disabilities, the focus in society shifts to people with disabilities as being equally able to participate in everyday life, and with said shift there are political and structural initiatives growing to help realize those rights. Countries which put the UN Convention into contracts are pioneers, however, proclaiming to promote the rights of people with disabilities isn't enough. Social actors are needed to create a framework that makes participation possible.
This article describes a fundamental qualitative attitude and it discusses methods already implemented in Germany'y elementary sector of education. The pathway to inclusion needs removal of barriers as well as the creation and expansion of benefit factors to turn participation into reality.

Wolfgang Heckmann

Dr. of Psychology, Prof. em. of Social Psychology and head of MISTEL, Institute at University of Applied Sciences Magdeburg-Stendal, Germany

A Meaningful Life After Recovering from Addiction –
Future After No Future

This is a reflection on practical experiences of more than 47 years in treating addicts, mainly opiate addicts. The focus is on the question, if - after a long time of lost meaning of life - a new start after treatment might lead to a meaningful life. Only very experienced therapists will be able to give an answer to this question. Most of not very much involved people believe in the sentence „Once an addict, always an addict". But those, who have seen quite a number of successfully treated or matured out and finally included former addicts, know better: A sober life after a history of addiction is possible. But there are two aspects, which are fundamental for the success after recovering from drug dependency:

Statisfactory abstinence. If this self-estimation does not occur, there will always be a risk for relapse and transcendence. It is for many therapists a surprise, that the need for transcendence is of great importance for the majority of former addicts.

Frances Anne McPherson

Dr. of Education of Exceptional Students, Professor in colleges of education at universities in Georgia, Michigan and South Carolina, USA. After her academic retirement she continued as advocate for disadvantaged and underrepresented youth to achieve higher education goals.

Meaningful Life in the United States - Social Rifts, Political Trends and Community Action

Meaningful life in the US has been put in jeopardy by deepening social rifts – aggravated by the current leadership's policies. White nationalism threatens civil liberties and human rights. Self-aggrandizement of a "Me First" agenda obstructs democracy and cripples social programs. An "America First" agenda isolates the nation, abandons global leadership agreements, jeopardizes international security and alienates democratic allies.

While most Americans agree on many issues, politicized fear-mongering polarizes them. Social rifts mirror political ideological divides regarding racism, immigration, abortion, gun control and criminal justice.

However, parts of society are stepping up community action to reinforce the rule of law, energize the democratic process, and empower disadvantaged populations. Advocacy groups representing civil liberties and human rights organize relief efforts, lobby legislators, mobilize protests, initiate boycotts and empower free speech.

Nina Rodefeld, Pascale Schinkitz, Aaron Schäfer
Bachelor-Students of Social Work at the University of Applied Sciences Magdeburg-Stendal, Germany

Digital Media First: A Comparison of German and Ukrainian Students

In June 2018, 11 students of the University of Applied Sciences Magdeburg-Stendal, Germany, visited the Ukrainian partner university „Gregorij Skovoroda"in Perejaslaw-Chmelnyzkyi. One part of the research was to conduct a small survey on the use of the media among Ukrainian students by the German visitors and among German students by the Ukrainians during their return visit in Germany. Findings are presented in this article. The main result consists of a striking similarity by the amount of time spent in the internet and with social media. Differences only refer to the social platforms and forums which are being used.

Lyudmyla Romanenkova
PhD., Docent at Classic Private University (CPU), Zaporizhzhya, and director of Zaporizhzhya Regional Non-government organization „Florence", Ukraine

The meaning of life and its significance in a difficult period of Ukrainian society

The article is devoted to the analyses of the meaning of life at different levels, including psychological and social context of the issue. The main focus is on the meaning of life for Ukrainian population in the context of military conflict between Ukraine and Russian and the consequences of the political decisions of Russia on Ukraine. Main research methods are statistical methods, interview and observation.

Fritz-Helmut Wisch
Dr. of Philosophy, Prof. em. of Special Education, University of Applied Sciences Magdeburg-Stendal, Germany

What 90 of my friends and relatives are thinking of a "meaningful life"

Answers that might bring us closer to the meaning of the term "meaningful life" can be found in the "commandment to love our neighbor", the "Golden Rule", and the ideals of the French revolution called "Freedom, Equality, and Brotherhood", the latter leading to human and civil rights and full sovereignty being granted for the people.

Due to the conference theme, the author asked 100 people about what it takes to have a "meaningful life". Some of the subjects that were deemed as "very important" comprised peace, freedom, health, education, honesty, humanity, democracy, family, love, and charity as well as friends, loyalty, tolerance, work, culture, having fun, having a beautiful home, travelling, hobbies and sports. In addition, the author presents key results of a study amongst the German population regarding ther expectations from the year 2010.

Jürgen Wolf
Sociologist, Dr. of Philosophy, Professor of Social Gerontology, University of Applied Sciences Magdeburg-Stendal, Germany

Meaningful Life in Old Age. Critical Thoughts on the „Active Ageing" Agenda

Like other Eastern European countries, Ukraine is confronted with a demographic change which results in a shrinking population and growing proportions of older people. Considering these developments, older people are a particularly vulnerable group who depend on welfare provisions and network resources to high degree. Thus, the measures of „active ageing" which are set by mainstream social gerontology and political programmes are inappropriate concepts for the Elderly in Ukraine. The author asks for alternative approaches to reach a meaningful life in old age by referring to thoughts of cultural gerontology and qualitative empirical findings from biographical interviews with older Ukrainian people.